Cuisinart Bread Machine Cookbook for Beginners

Healthy and Delicious Recipes, Including Gluten-Free and Whole Grain Options, Perfect for Home Baking Enthusiasts and Bread Lovers.

Zowena Bendilety

Table of Contents

INTRODUCTION

Things You Need to Know About Your Cuisinart Bread Machine

Your Cuisinart bread machine is a versatile kitchen appliance designed to simplify the bread-making process while offering a range of customizable options to suit your preferences. Here are some essential things you need to know about your bread machine to make the most out of it:

Preprogrammed Menu Options: The bread machine comes with 12 preprogrammed menu options, making it easy to bake a variety of bread types, including gluten-free and artisan breads. These options take the guesswork out of bread making, ensuring consistent results every time.

Customizable Crust Colors and Loaf Sizes: Whether you prefer a light, medium, or dark crust, or need a smaller or larger loaf size, your bread machine can accommodate your preferences. With three crust shades and three loaf sizes (1, 1.5, and 2 pounds), you have the flexibility to tailor your bread to your liking.

Delay-Start Timer: The 13-hour delay-start timer allows you to set your bread machine to start baking at a later time, so you can wake up to the irresistible aroma of freshly baked bread. This feature is convenient for busy schedules or when you want to have bread ready for a specific time.

Versatility Beyond Bread: While the primary function of the bread machine is to

bake bread, it can also be used to make other treats like cakes and pizza dough. Experiment with different recipes to discover the full potential of your bread machine and delight your family and friends with homemade goodies.

Easy Monitoring and Cleanup: The bread machine is designed for convenience, with features like a viewing window and interior light that allow you to monitor the baking process without interrupting it. Additionally, the removable kneading paddle and bread pan make cleanup a breeze, ensuring that you can enjoy your freshly baked bread without the hassle of scrubbing.

LCD Display: The easy-to-read LED display provides clear information about the countdown time, current cycle, and selected options. This allows you to track the progress of your bread and make any necessary adjustments to ensure optimal results.

Power Failure Backup: Worried about power outages ruining your baking efforts? Fear not, as your bread machine is equipped with a power failure backup feature, ensuring that your bread will continue baking uninterrupted even if the power goes out temporarily.

BPA-Free Construction: Your bread machine is made with BPA-free materials, giving you peace of mind about the safety of your food. This commitment to health and safety is a testament to Cuisinart's dedication to quality and innovation.

Warranty: Enjoy the confidence of a limited 3-year warranty, knowing that your bread machine is backed by Cuisinart's commitment to quality and customer

satisfaction. This warranty provides added reassurance and support in case of any issues with your appliance.

User-Friendly Features: From audible reminders to indicate when to remove the paddle or add mix-ins, to a keep warm cycle that ensures your bread stays fresh until you're ready to enjoy it, your bread machine is designed with user convenience in mind. These thoughtful features make the bread-making process seamless and enjoyable for both novice and experienced bakers alike.

In conclusion, your Cuisinart bread machine is more than just a kitchen appliance—it's a versatile tool that empowers you to bake a wide range of delicious breads and treats with ease. By familiarizing yourself with its features and capabilities, you can unlock endless possibilities for culinary creativity and enjoyment in your kitchen.

Tips For Successful Bread Making with Cuisinart Machines

Successful bread making with a Cuisinart bread machine can be an immensely rewarding experience, but like any culinary endeavor, it requires attention

to detail and a good understanding of the machine's features. Here are some tips to help you make the most of your Cuisinart bread maker:

Follow the Recipe: This might seem obvious, but it's worth emphasizing. Always follow the recipe provided in the Cuisinart recipe book or one specifically tailored for bread machines. These recipes are formulated to work well with the machine's settings and ensure consistent results.

Measure Ingredients Accurately: Baking is a science, and even small discrepancies in ingredient measurements can affect the final outcome. Use measuring cups and spoons designed for dry and liquid ingredients, and level off ingredients like flour and sugar for precise measurements.

Use Fresh Ingredients: Quality ingredients are key to great-tasting bread. Use fresh flour, yeast, and other ingredients to ensure optimal results. Check the expiration date on your yeast and store it in a cool, dry place to maintain its potency.

Experiment with Flours: While all-purpose flour is commonly used in bread making, don't be afraid to experiment with different types of flour, such as whole wheat, rye, or spelt. Each type of flour will impart its own unique flavor and texture to the bread.

Understand Your Machine's Settings: Familiarize yourself with the settings on your Cuisinart bread machine, including crust color, loaf size, and program options. Understanding how each setting affects the final product will allow you to customize your bread to your preferences.

Prep Ingredients Properly: Some recipes may require prepping ingredients

before adding them to the bread machine. For example, if you're adding nuts, seeds, or dried fruit, chop them into small pieces to ensure even distribution throughout the bread.

Don't Overload the Machine: It can be tempting to pack in as many ingredients as possible, but overloading the bread machine can lead to uneven baking and potentially a collapsed loaf. Follow the manufacturer's recommendations for maximum ingredient quantities.

Monitor the Dough: Pay attention to the dough as it kneads and rises in the machine. If the dough appears too dry or too wet, adjust the recipe by adding a little more flour or water until you achieve the desired consistency.

Customize Recipes: Once you've mastered basic bread recipes, don't hesitate to get creative and experiment with different flavors and ingredients. Add herbs, spices, cheese, or even chocolate chips to create unique bread varieties.

Practice Patience: Good bread takes time, so don't rush the process. Allow the bread machine to complete each stage of the baking cycle, including kneading, rising, and baking, without interruption. Resist the temptation to open the lid

● Jalapeño Cheddar Bread

● Ciabatta

● Cinnamon Swirl Rolls

● Multigrain Bread

during baking, as this can disrupt the baking process.

By following these tips and experimenting with different recipes, you'll soon become a master bread maker with your Cuisinart bread machine. Enjoy the process and savor the delicious homemade bread that awaits you!

How to Make Gluten-Free and Whole Grain Bread

Making gluten-free and whole grain bread in your Cuisinart Bread Machine is a breeze, thanks to its versatile settings and foolproof recipes. Here's a comprehensive guide to creating delicious gluten-free and whole grain loaves that will tantalize your taste buds:

Choose the Right Ingredients: The key to successful gluten-free and whole grain bread lies in selecting the right ingredients. Opt for gluten-free flour blends or whole grain flours like brown rice flour, oat flour, quinoa flour, or almond flour. These alternatives provide nutrients and fiber while avoiding gluten.

Follow a Recipe: While the Cuisinart Bread Machine comes with pre-programmed options, it's essential to use recipes specifically formulated for gluten-free or whole grain bread. These recipes typically require additional moisture and binding agents to compensate for the lack of gluten. Follow the measurements and instructions carefully to ensure the best results.

Adjust Liquid Content: Gluten-free flours tend to absorb more moisture than traditional wheat flour. Therefore, you may need to adjust the liquid content of your recipe accordingly. Start with the recommended amount of liquid and observe the dough's consistency during the kneading cycle. If the dough appears too dry or crumbly, add a tablespoon of liquid at a time until you achieve the desired texture.

Incorporate Binding Agents: Since gluten is responsible for giving bread its structure and elasticity, gluten-free bread requires additional binding agents to hold the dough together. Common binding agents include xanthan gum, guar gum, or psyllium husk powder. These ingredients help prevent the bread from crumbling and ensure a soft, cohesive texture.

Experiment with Flavors and Add-Ins: Enhance the flavor and texture of your gluten-free or whole grain bread by incorporating various add-ins such as seeds, nuts, dried fruits, or herbs. These ingredients not only contribute to the nutritional value of the bread but also add complexity to its taste profile. Experiment with different combinations to find your perfect blend.

Select the Appropriate Cycle: When using the Cuisinart Bread Machine, choose the appropriate cycle for gluten-free or whole grain bread. These cycles are designed to accommodate the specific needs of these types of bread, including longer kneading and rising times. Refer to the instruction manual for guidance on selecting the correct cycle for your recipe.

Monitor the Process: While the bread machine takes care of the mixing, kneading, rising, and baking, it's essential to monitor the process, especially during the initial stages. Check the dough's consistency during the kneading cycle, ensuring it forms a smooth, elastic ball. Additionally, keep an eye on the rising progress to prevent the dough from overflowing the pan.

Customize Crust and Loaf Size: The Cuisinart Bread Machine offers customizable

options for crust color and loaf size. Select your preferred crust shade – light, medium, or dark – and choose the appropriate loaf size based on your needs. Whether you prefer a small loaf for personal consumption or a larger one for sharing, the bread machine can accommodate your preferences.

Enjoy Freshly Baked Bread: Once the baking cycle is complete, remove the bread from the machine and let it cool on a wire rack before slicing. The aroma of freshly baked gluten-free or whole grain bread will fill your kitchen, enticing you to indulge in a slice or two. Serve it warm with your favorite spreads or enjoy it as a standalone treat.

Store Properly: To maintain the freshness and quality of your gluten-free or whole grain bread, store it in an airtight container or resealable bag at room temperature. Homemade bread is best consumed within a few days, but you can also freeze individual slices for longer-term storage. Simply thaw them as needed and toast or reheat for a quick and delicious snack.

With these tips and techniques, you can confidently make gluten-free and whole grain bread in your Cuisinart Bread Machine, elevating your baking repertoire and satisfying your cravings for wholesome homemade goodness. Experiment with different recipes and ingredients to discover new flavors and textures, and enjoy the satisfaction of baking bread from scratch in the comfort of your own kitchen.

Common Bread-making Issues With Cuisinart Machines

Cuisinart bread machines are renowned for their versatility and ease of use, but like any kitchen appliance, they can encounter common issues that may affect the bread-making process. Here, we delve into some of these potential challenges and provide troubleshooting tips to help you get the most out of your Cuisinart bread machine.

Uneven Rising or Dense Loaves:

One of the most common issues encountered when using a bread machine is bread that doesn't rise properly or turns out dense. Several factors could contribute to this problem:

Expired Yeast: Ensure that your yeast is fresh and not expired. Expired yeast can lead to poor rising.

Water Temperature: The water used in the recipe should be at the correct temperature specified in the recipe instructions. Too hot or too cold water can affect yeast activation and subsequent rising.

Inadequate Kneading: If the dough is not kneaded properly, it won't develop enough gluten, resulting in a dense loaf. Make sure the kneading paddle is properly attached and functioning.

Improper Measurement of Ingredients: Accurate measurement of ingredients is crucial in bread-making. Use measuring cups and spoons designed for dry and wet ingredients respectively, and level off the excess for precise measurements.

High Altitude: If you live at a high altitude, you may need to adjust the recipes accordingly. High altitudes can affect rising times and may require modifications to the amount of yeast or liquid used.

To address these issues, double-check your ingredients, water temperature, and ensure that the kneading process is adequate. Experiment with adjustments to the recipe for high-altitude baking if necessary.

Crust Too Dark or Too Light:

Achieving the perfect crust color can be challenging, but it's essential for the overall taste and appearance of the bread. Here are some reasons why your crust might not be turning out as desired:

Crust Setting: Make sure you have selected the appropriate crust setting (light, medium, or dark) based on your preference. Adjust the setting as needed for future bakes.

Placement in the Machine: The position of the bread pan within the machine can affect crust color. Ensure it is centered for even baking.

Overbaking: If the crust is consistently too dark, try reducing the baking time slightly. Conversely, if it's too light, increase the baking time gradually until you achieve the desired color.

External Factors: Ambient temperature and humidity can also impact crust color. Try to bake in a consistent environment to maintain control over the baking process.

Experiment with different settings and keep a close eye on the crust during baking to make adjustments as needed.

Stuck Bread or Paddle:

Another common issue with bread machines is bread or the kneading paddle sticking to the pan, making it difficult to remove. Here's how to address this problem:

Grease the Pan: Ensure that the bread pan is adequately greased before adding the ingredients. Use a non-stick cooking spray or brush the pan with oil to prevent sticking.

Check Kneading Paddle: Make sure the kneading paddle is properly attached to the shaft and that there are no obstructions preventing it from moving freely during the kneading process.

Remove Promptly: Once the baking cycle is complete, promptly remove the bread from the pan to prevent it from sticking as it cools.

Use the Right Pan: Some bread machines offer the option to use different types of pans, such as non-stick or stainless steel. Choose the one that works best for your recipes and preferences.

Taking these precautions can help minimize the likelihood of bread sticking to the pan or paddle, ensuring easy removal and cleanup.

Unexpected Beeping or Error Codes:

If your Cuisinart bread machine emits unexpected beeping sounds or displays error codes during operation, it could indicate various issues:

Power Interruptions: Beeping sounds or error codes may occur if there's a power interruption during the baking process. Check the power source and ensure it's stable throughout the baking cycle.

Overloading: Avoid overloading the bread machine with ingredients beyond its capacity, as this can trigger error codes or malfunctions. Stick to the recommended maximum amounts for each recipe.

Technical Malfunctions: If the bread machine continues to display error codes or malfunction despite troubleshooting, refer to the user manual for specific instructions on how to address technical issues. You may need to contact customer support or seek professional assistance for repairs.

It's essential to follow the manufacturer's guidelines for troubleshooting and maintenance to ensure optimal performance and longevity of your Cuisinart bread machine.

In conclusion, while Cuisinart bread machines offer convenience and versatility in home baking, they may encounter common issues such as uneven rising, crust color problems, sticking, or error codes. By following proper troubleshooting steps, including verifying ingredients, adjusting settings, and maintaining the machine, you can overcome these challenges and enjoy delicious homemade bread with your Cuisinart bread maker.

Basic Knowledge for A Novice

If you're new to the world of bread making or using a bread machine, there are a few basic concepts and tips that can help you get started on your journey to becoming a home baker extraordinaire. Let's delve into the foundational knowledge for a novice bread maker:

Understanding Ingredients:

Before you start baking, it's essential to understand the basic ingredients that go into making bread:

Flour: Flour provides the structure for your bread. All-purpose flour is

commonly used for most bread recipes, but you can also experiment with whole wheat, rye, or other specialty flours for different flavors and textures.

Yeast: Yeast is the microorganism responsible for fermentation, which gives bread its rise and airy texture. Active dry yeast or instant yeast are the most common types used in bread making. It's essential to activate the yeast properly by dissolving it in warm water or milk with a pinch of sugar before adding it to the rest of the ingredients.

Liquid: Water is the most common liquid used in bread making, but you can also use milk or other dairy-free alternatives. The liquid hydrates the flour and activates the yeast.

Salt: Salt not only enhances the flavor of the bread but also helps to regulate the fermentation process and strengthen the gluten structure.

Sweeteners: Sugar, honey, or other sweeteners can be added to bread dough to enhance flavor and promote yeast activity. However, too much sugar can inhibit yeast fermentation, so it's essential to use it in moderation.

Fats: Fats like butter, oil, or shortening add richness and moisture to the bread. They also help to tenderize the crumb and extend the shelf life of the loaf.

Basic Techniques:

Once you understand the ingredients, it's time to familiarize yourself with the basic techniques involved in bread making:

Mixing: In bread machines, the mixing is done automatically by the machine. However, if you're making bread by hand or using a stand mixer, you'll need to mix the ingredients until they form a cohesive dough.

Kneading: Kneading

develops the gluten in the flour, which gives the bread its structure and elasticity. If you're using a bread machine, the kneading is done by the machine's paddle. If kneading by hand, you'll need to knead the dough on a floured surface until it's smooth and elastic.

Rising: After kneading, the dough needs to rise to allow the yeast to ferment and create carbon dioxide bubbles, which give the bread its airy texture. This typically takes place in two stages: the first rise (bulk fermentation) and the second rise (proofing). In a bread machine, the rising is done automatically in the baking chamber.

Baking: Once the dough has risen, it's time to bake it. In a bread machine, this is done automatically according to the selected program. If baking in an oven, preheat the oven to the specified temperature and bake the bread until it's golden brown and sounds hollow when tapped on the bottom.

By understanding the basic ingredients, techniques, and tips outlined above, you'll be well-equipped to embark on your bread making journey with confidence, whether using a bread machine or baking by hand. Happy baking!

Chapter 1: Basic breads

Softest Soft Bread with Air Pockets Using Bread Machine

Prep Time: 10 mins   Cook Time: 55 mins
Additional Time: 2 hrs 10 mins   Serves: 8

Ingredients:

- 1 cup warm water (105 to115 degrees f)
- 4 tsps honey
- 2 tsps active dry yeast
- 2 cups all-purpose flour
- 4 tsps olive oil
- ½ tsp salt

Directions:

1. Pour warm water into the pan of a bread machine and stir in honey until dissolved. Add yeast; let stand until foamy, about 10 minutes.
2. Add flour, olive oil, and salt to the pan in the order listed or follow the order recommended by the manufacturer if different.
3. Run the White cycle.
4. Remove loaf from the machine after the cycle is done, about 55 minutes. Allow baked loaf to cool before slicing.

Nutritional Value (Amount per Serving):

Calories: 172; Fat: 3.41; Carb: 31.15; Protein: 4.71

Steakhouse Wheat Bread for the Bread Machine

Prep Time: 10 mins   Cook Time: 3 hrs   Serves: 8

Ingredients:

- ¾ cup warm water
- 1 tbsp butter, softened
- ¼ cup honey
- ½ tsp salt
- 1 tsp instant coffee granules
- 1 tbsp unsweetened cocoa powder
- 1 tbsp white sugar
- 1 cup bread flour
- 1 cup whole wheat flour
- 1 ¼ tsps bread machine yeast

Directions:

1. Place warm water, butter, honey, salt, coffee, cocoa, sugar, bread flour, whole wheat flour, and bread machine yeast in the pan of a bread machine in the order listed.
2. Put on the White cycle with light crust.
3. Remove loaf from the machine after the cycle is done. Allow baked loaf to cool before slicing.

Nutritional Value (Amount per Serving):

Calories: 164; Fat: 2.28; Carb: 32.85; Protein: 4.75

Herb Bread for Bread Machine

Prep Time: 10 mins   Cook Time: 3 hrs   Serves: 8

Ingredients:

- 1 cup warm water
- 1 egg, beaten
- 1 tsp salt
- 2 tbsps white sugar
- 2 tbsps extra-virgin olive oil
- 2 tsps dried rosemary leaves, crushed
- 1 tsp dried oregano
- 1 tsp dried basil
- 3 cups all-purpose flour
- 2 tbsps all-purpose flour
- 2 tsps bread machine yeast

Directions:

1. Pour warm water into the pan of your bread machine; add egg, salt, white sugar, olive oil, rosemary, oregano, basil, flour, and bread machine yeast, respectively.
2. Set machine to Bake with light crust and press start.
3. Remove the bread from the machine with oven mitts after the cycle is done, and allow it to cool before slicing.

Nutritional Value (Amount per Serving):

Calories: 245; Fat: 3.7; Carb: 45.27; Protein: 7.4

Ron's Bread Machine White

Prep Time: 5 mins   Cook Time: 3 hrs   Serves: 15

Ingredients:

- 1 cup water
- 1 extra large egg, beaten
- 2 tbsps dry milk powder
- 1 tbsp white sugar
- 2 tbsps vegetable oil
- 1 ½ tsps salt
- 1 cup bread flour
- 2 cups all-purpose flour
- 1 ¼ tsps active dry yeast

Directions:

1. Place ingredients in order suggested by your manufacturer.
2. Select the White setting, medium crust.
3. Remove loaf from the machine with oven mitts after the cycle is done. Allow the bread to cool before slicing.

Nutritional Value (Amount per Serving):

Calories: 122; Fat: 2.37; Carb: 21.55; Protein: 3.48

Bread Machine Pumpernickel Bread

Prep Time: 10 mins   Cook Time: 12 mins   Serves: 12

Ingredients:

- 1 ⅛ cups warm water
- 1 ½ tbsps vegetable oil
- ⅓ cup molasses
- 3 tbsps cocoa
- 1 tbsp caraway seed (optional)
- 1 ½ tsps salt
- 1 ½ cups bread flour
- 1 cup rye flour
- 1 cup whole wheat flour
- 1 ½ tbsps vital wheat gluten (optional)
- 2 ½ tsps bread machine yeast

Directions:

1. Place ingredients in the pan of the bread machine in the order recommended by the manufacturer. Select the White cycle; press start.
2. Remove the bread from the machine with oven mitts after the cycle is done, and allow it to cool before slicing.

Nutritional Value (Amount per Serving):

Calories: 195; Fat: 2.69; Carb: 36.63; Protein: 6.99

Bread Machine – Italian Herb Bread

Prep Time: 5 mins   Cook Time: 3 hrs   Serves: 12

Ingredients:

- 1 1/8 cups milk (lukewarm)
- 4 tbsps unsalted butter (softened)
- 3 cups bread flour (not all purpose flour)
- 1 1/2 tbsps white granulated sugar
- 1 tbsp Italian herbs seasoning
- 1/2 tsp onion powder (optional)
- 1 tsp salt
- 1 tsp bread machine yeast

Directions:

1. Pour the milk into the bread pan and then add the other ingredients (including the italian herb seasoning). Place the bread machine yeast in last and the yeast should not touch the liquid (until the bread machine is turned on and the ingredients start to be mixed together).
2. Enter the correct settings into your bread machine (1.5 lb, light crust & White setting) and press the "Start" Button.
3. After the bread machine has finished baking the bread, unplug the bread machine. Remove the bread from the bread pan and place it on a cooling rack. Use oven mitts when removing the bread pan from the bread machine as it will be very hot!

Nutritional Value (Amount per Serving):

Calories: 172; Fat: 4.01; Carb: 28.26; Protein: 5.27

Bread Machine Almond Bread

Prep Time: 10 mins   Cook Time: 3 hrs   Serves: 12

Ingredients:

- 1 ¼ cups water
- ¼ cup honey
- 4 tsps almond oil
- 1 tsp salt
- 2 cups whole wheat flour
- 1 cup almond flour
- ¼ cup vital wheat gluten
- 1 tsp xanthan gum
- 1 (0.25 oz.) package dry yeast

Directions:

1. Combine water, honey, almond oil, salt, whole wheat flour, almond flour, vital wheat gluten, xanthan gum, and yeast in a bread machine.
2. Select the White setting with a 2 lb loaf.
3. Remove the pan from the machine. Allow bread to cool completely before slicing.

Nutritional Value (Amount per Serving):

Calories: 141; Fat: 3.26; Carb: 22.76; Protein: 7.43

Rosemary Herb Bread

Prep Time: 5 mins   Cook Time: 3 hrs   Serves: 12

Ingredients:

- ⅔ cup milk
- 2 eggs
- 3 cups bread flour
- 1 ½ tsps salt
- 2 ½ tbsps white sugar
- 1 tsp chopped fresh rosemary
- 1 tsp chopped fresh thyme
- 1 tsp dried marjoram
- 1 ½ tbsps margarine
- 2 tsps active dry yeast

Directions:

1. Place ingredients in the bread machine in the order suggested by the manufacture.
2. Select White setting. Start.
3. Remove loaf from the machine after the cycle is done and allow it to cool before slicing.

Nutritional Value (Amount per Serving):

Calories: 186; Fat: 4.23; Carb: 29.65; Protein: 7

Bread Machine Irish Soda Bread

Prep Time: 5 mins   Cook Time: 2 hrs 55 mins   Serves: 12

Ingredients:

- 1 ½ cups warm water (110 degrees f)
- 2 tbsps margarine
- 2 tbsps white sugar
- 1 tsp salt
- 4 ¼ cups bread flour
- 2 tbsps dry milk powder
- 3 tsps caraway seed
- 2 tsps active dry yeast
- ⅔ cup raisins

Directions:

1. Place warm water, margarine, sugar, salt, bread flour, milk powder, caraway seed, and yeast into a bread machine in the order listed, or follow the order recommended by the manufacturer if different.
2. Run the White cycle, adding raisins when indicated.
3. Remove loaf from the machine after the cycle is done, about 2 hours 55 minutes.

Nutritional Value (Amount per Serving):

Calories: 230; Fat: 3.4; Carb: 42.42; Protein: 7.7

Flax and Sunflower Seed Bread

Prep Time: 10 mins   Cook Time: 3 hrs   Serves: 15

Ingredients:

- 1 ⅓ cups water
- 2 tbsps butter, softened
- 3 tbsps honey
- 1 ½ cups bread flour
- 1 ⅓ cups whole wheat bread flour
- 1 tsp salt
- 1 tsp active dry yeast
- ½ cup flax seeds
- ½ cup sunflower seeds

Directions:

1. Place all ingredients (except sunflower seeds) in the pan of the bread machine in the order recommended by the manufacturer.
2. Select the White cycle; press start.
3. Add the sunflower seeds when the alert sounds during the knead cycle.
4. Remove loaf from the machine after the cycle is done, and allow it to cool completely.

Nutritional Value (Amount per Serving):

Calories: 178; Fat: 7.29; Carb: 22.81; Protein: 6.21

Dark Rye Bread

Prep Time: 15 mins   Cook Time: 3 hrs   Serves: 12

Ingredients:

- 1 ⅛ cups water
- 2 tbsps molasses
- 1 tbsp vegetable oil
- 1 tsp salt
- 2 cups all-purpose flour
- 1 ½ cups rye flour
- 3 tbsps packed brown sugar
- 1 tbsp unsweetened cocoa powder
- ¾ tsp caraway seed
- 2 tsps bread machine yeast

Directions:

1. Place ingredients in the pan of the bread machine in the order recommended by the manufacturer.
2. Select the White cycle, and press start.
3. After the baking cycle ends, remove bread from pan, place on a cake rack, and allow to cool completely before slicing.

Nutritional Value (Amount per Serving):

Calories: 157; Fat: 1.63; Carb: 31.63; Protein: 4.21

Danish Rugbrod for the Bread Machine

Prep Time: 10 mins   Cook Time: 3 hrs   Serves: 24

Ingredients:

- 1 ½ cups water
- 1 tbsp honey
- 1 tbsp butter
- 1 tsp salt
- 2 cups rye flour
- 2 tsps bread machine yeast
- 1 cup all-purpose flour
- 1 cup whole wheat flour
- ¼ cup rye flakes (optional)
- 1 tbsp white sugar

Directions:

1. Put water, honey, butter, salt, rye flour, all-purpose flour, whole wheat flour, rye flakes, sugar, and yeast, respectively, into the pan of your bread machine.
2. Select White setting and press start.
3. Remove bread from pan, place on a cake rack, and allow to cool completely before slicing.

Nutritional Value (Amount per Serving):

Calories: 79; Fat: 0.84; Carb: 15.76; Protein: 2.53

Bread Machine Sugar-Free Bread

Prep Time: 15 mins   Cook Time: 1 hr   Serves: 15

Ingredients:

- 1 (0.25 oz.) package active dry yeast
- 1 cup skim milk, luke warm
- 2 tbsps warm water (110 degrees f)
- ½ tsp salt
- 2 cups all-purpose flour
- 1 ¼ cups whole wheat flour
- 1 tbsp olive oil

Directions:

1. Place ingredients in the pan of the bread machine in the order recommended by the manufacturer. Select White setting; press start.
2. Remove bread from pan, place on a cake rack, and allow to cool completely before slicing.

Nutritional Value (Amount per Serving):

Calories: 115; Fat: 1.36; Carb: 22.23; Protein: 3.75

Light Oat Bread

Prep Time: 5 mins
Additional Time: 2 hrs

Cook Time: 55 mins
Serves: 12

Ingredients:

- 1 ¼ cups water
- 2 tbsps margarine
- 1 tsp salt
- 3 cups all-purpose flour
- ½ cup rolled oats
- 2 tbsps brown sugar
- 1 ½ tsps active dry yeast

Directions:

1. Place water, margarine, salt, flour, oats, brown sugar, and yeast into a bread machine in the order listed, or follow the order recommended by your manufacturer if different.
2. Select White setting.
3. Remove loaf from the machine after the cycle is done and allow it to completely cool.

Nutritional Value (Amount per Serving):

Calories: 155; Fat: 2.61; Carb: 29.55; Protein: 4.63

Amish Bread

Prep Time: 5 mins   Cook Time: 55 mins
Additional Time 4 hrs   Serves: 12

Ingredients:

- 2 ¾ cups bread flour
- ¼ cup canola oil
- 1 tsp active dry yeast
- ¼ cup white sugar
- ½ tsp salt
- 1 ⅛ cups warm water, or more as needed

Directions:

1. Place flour, oil, yeast, sugar, salt, and warm water into a bread machine in the order listed, or follow the order recommended by your manufacturer if different.
2. Select White cycle.
3. When dough has gone through one rise cycle and the second kneading cycle is beginning, turn the machine off. Select White cycle again, this time letting it go through the full cycle.
4. Remove loaf from the machine after the cycle is done.

Nutritional Value (Amount per Serving):

Calories: 164; Fat: 5.89; Carb: 23.44; Protein: 4.02

Buttermilk Wheat Bread

Prep Time: 8 mins   Cook Time: 6 hrs   Serves: 12

Ingredients:

- 1 ½ cups buttermilk
- 1 ½ tbsps butter, melted
- 2 tbsps white sugar
- ¾ tsp salt
- 3 cups all-purpose flour
- ⅓ cup whole wheat flour
- 1 ½ tsps active dry yeast

Directions:

1. Place all ingredients into a bread machine in the order recommended by the manufacturer.
2. Select the White setting, then press start. If the ingredients do not form a ball after a few minutes, add a splash more buttermilk, or a handful of flour if it is too loose.
3. Remove loaf from the machine after the cycle is done and allow it to cool completely before slicing.

Nutritional Value (Amount per Serving):

Calories: 165; Fat: 2.23; Carb: 30.78; Protein: 5.41

White Bread I

Prep Time: 5 mins   Cook Time: 3 hrs   Serves: 12

Ingredients:

- 1 ¼ cups lukewarm milk
- 3 cups all-purpose flour
- 1 ½ tbsps white sugar
- 1 ½ tsps salt
- 2 tbsps butter
- 2 tsps active dry yeast

Directions:

1. Place ingredients in the pan of the bread machine in the order suggested by the manufacturer.
2. Select White setting, and press start.
3. When done, place on wire rack for at least 10 minutes before slicing.

Nutritional Value (Amount per Serving):

Calories: 158; Fat: 2.91; Carb: 27.81; Protein: 5.04

Milk Bread

Prep Time: 5 mins
Additional Time: 1 hr 25 mins

Cook Time: 30 mins
Serves: 15

Ingredients:

- 1 ⅛ cups milk
- 3 cups all-purpose flour
- 1 tsp salt
- 3 tbsps white sugar
- 1 ½ tsps active dry yeast

Directions:

1. Place ingredients in the pan of the bread machine in the order recommended by the manufacturer. Select White cycle; press start.
2. Remove loaf from the machine after the cycle is done and allow it to cool before slicing.

Nutritional Value (Amount per Serving):

Calories: 118; Fat: 0.95; Carb: 23.37; Protein: 3.74

Buttermilk Honey Wheat Bread

Prep Time: 5 mins   Cook Time: 3 hrs 3 mins   Serves: 12

Ingredients:

- 2 ½ tsps active dry yeast
- 1 cup whole wheat flour
- 2 cups all-purpose flour
- ½ tsp baking soda
- 1 tsp salt
- 3 tbsps honey
- 1 ½ tbsps vegetable oil
- 1 ½ cups buttermilk, at room temperature

Directions:

1. Combine the yeast, whole wheat flour, all purpose flour, baking soda, salt, honey, oil, and buttermilk into pan of a bread machine.
2. Use medium crust and White setting.
3. Remove loaf from the machine after the cycle is done and allow it to cool before slicing.

Nutritional Value (Amount per Serving):

Calories: 158; Fat: 2.72; Carb: 28.7; Protein: 5.69

Simple Homemade Whole Wheat Honey Bread

Prep Time: 5 mins   Cook Time: 3 hrs   Serves: 12

Ingredients:

- 1 ⅛ cups water
- 3 cups whole wheat flour
- 1 ½ tsps salt
- ⅓ cup honey
- 1 tbsp dry milk powder
- 1 ½ tbsps shortening
- 1 ½ tsps active dry yeast

Directions:

1. Place ingredients in bread machine pan in the order suggested by the manufacturer.
2. Select Whole Wheat setting, and then press start.
3. Remove loaf from the machine after the cycle is done and allow it to cool before slicing.

Nutritional Value (Amount per Serving):

Calories: 156; Fat: 2.66; Carb: 30.96; Protein: 4.81

Oatmeal Bread II

Prep Time: 5 mins   Cook Time: 3 hrs   Serves: 12

Ingredients:

- 1 ¼ cups water
- 3 cups bread flour
- 2 tbsps honey
- 1 ½ tbsps dry milk powder

- 1 ½ tsps salt
- ½ cup quick cooking oats
- 2 tbsps margarine
- 1 tbsp active dry yeast

Directions:

1. Place ingredients in the pan of the bread machine in the order recommended by the manufacturer. Select White setting, and start.
2. Remove loaf from the machine after the cycle is done and allow it to cool before slicing.

Nutritional Value (Amount per Serving):

Calories: 165; Fat: 2.99; Carb: 28.72; Protein: 5.58

Super Easy Rosemary Bread Machine Bread

Prep Time: 10 mins   Cook Time: 3 hrs   Serves: 6

Ingredients:

- 1 cup warm water (110 degrees f)
- 2 ½ tsps active dry yeast
- 3 tbsps white sugar
- 1 ½ tsps salt
- 3 tbsps olive oil
- ½ tsp ground thyme
- ½ tsp garlic powder
- 2 tsps crushed dried rosemary
- 3 cups all-purpose flour

Directions:

1. Pour the water into the pan of a bread machine, then sprinkle in the yeast and sugar.
2. Let the mixture sit in the bread machine until a creamy foam forms on top of the water, about 10 minutes.
3. Sprinkle in the salt, then add olive oil, thyme, garlic powder, rosemary, and flour.
4. Set the machine for the White and light crust settings, and start the machine.
5. Once baked, remove the loaf from the pan and set it on a wire rack to cool completely.

Nutritional Value (Amount per Serving):

Calories: 316; Fat: 4.62; Carb: 60.44; Protein: 9.15

Bread Machine - Bacon Bread

Prep Time: 5 mins   Cook Time: 3 hrs   Serves: 12

Ingredients:

- 1 1/3 cups water (warm)
- 4 tbsps butter (sliced)

- 3 cups bread flour
- 1 cup one minute oatmeal
- 1 tsp salt
- 1/4 cup dark brown sugar
- 1 1/2 tsp bread machine yeast
- 4 tbsps bacon bits

Directions:

1. Add all ingredients (except the bacon bits) starting with the water into the bread machine "bucket" (loaf pan). Place the bread machine yeast in last and the yeast should not touch the water (until the bread machine is turned on and the ingredients start to be mixed together).
2. Enter the correct settings (2lb, light color and White) and press "Start" Button.
3. After the bread machine has finished its first kneading cycle, add the bacon bits. You can add them with the other ingredients, but the bacon bits will be more broken up and very small if they go through two kneading cycles. Wear oven mitts.
4. After the bread machine has finished its final kneading cycle and before the baking cycle starts, gently sprinkle on some bacon bits on top of the dough. Wear oven mitts.
5. After the bread machine has finished baking the bread, remove the bread and place it on a cooling rack. Use oven mitts when removing the bread machine container as it will be very hot!

Nutritional Value (Amount per Serving):

Calories: 205; Fat: 5.83; Carb: 31.6; Protein: 6.27

High Fiber Bread Recipe

Prep Time: 2 hrs 45 mins   Cook Time: 40 mins   Serves: 18

Ingredients:

- 1 1/4 cups milk (warm)
- 4 tbsps unsalted butter (softened)
- 2 1/2 cups whole wheat flour
- 1 cup golden flaxseed meal – it can also be called finely ground golden flaxseed, ground golden flaxseed meal, etc. You want to use ground-up seeds and not whole seeds.
- 1/3 cup light brown sugar
- 1 1/2 tsps salt
- 1 1/2 tsps instant yeast (or bread machine yeast) – this recipe does not use active dry yeast.

Directions:

1. Soften the butter.
2. Pour the milk & softened butter into the bread pan and then add the other

ingredients. Place the instant yeast/bread machine yeast in last and the yeast should not touch the liquid (until the bread machine is turned on and the ingredients start to be mixed together by the bread machine).

3. Enter the correct settings (2 lb, light crust, White) and press the "Start" Button.
4. When the bread machine has finished baking the bread, unplug the bread machine and remove the bread pan from the bread machine. Wear oven mitts as the bread pan & bread machine will be hot.
5. Remove the bread from the bread pan and place the bread on a wire cooling rack. Use oven mitts when removing the bread as the bread & bread pan will be hot.
6. Optional (but recommended) – right after removing the bread from the bread pan (while the bread is still very hot), brush on 1 or 2 tbsps of melted butter on the top crust of the bread. This creates a more buttery top to the bread. Use a pastry brush to brush on the butter.
7. Let the bread cool on the wire cooling rack for 1-2 hours before cutting.

Nutritional Value (Amount per Serving):

Calories: 165; Fat: 9.29; Carb: 17.05; Protein: 5.74

Chapter 2: Sourdough Breads

Plain and Simple Sourdough Bread

Prep Time: 5 mins   Cook Time: 3 hrs   Serves: 12

Ingredients:

- ¾ cup warm water (110 degrees f)
- 1 cup sourdough starter
- 1 ½ tsps salt
- 2 ⅔ cups bread flour
- 1 ½ tsps active dry yeast

Directions:

1. Add all ingredients in order suggested by your manufacturer.
2. Select White setting and push start.
3. Cool the loaf once it's done.
4. Enjoy!

Nutritional Value (Amount per Serving):

Calories: 167; Fat: 1.1; Carb: 32.65; Protein: 6.4

Super Easy Bread Machine Sourdough Bread

Prep Time: 20 mins   Cook Time: 3 hrs   Serves: 12

Ingredients:

- 1 cup water (warm)
- 1/2 cup sourdough starter – you need to add live sourdough starter (not dry starter) to the bread pan. The starter should not be very liquidy. It should look like bubbly dough.
- 4 tbsps vegetable oil
- 2 1/2 cups bread flour
- 1/2 cup whole wheat flour
- 1 tbsp white granulated sugar
- 1 tsp salt
- 1 tsp bread machine yeast

Directions:

1. Measure the sourdough starter and stir out any bubbles (if you can). This helps to make the volume more consistent (versus including the volume of "Empty" Bubbles).
2. Pour the water, sourdough starter & oil into the bread pan first and then add the other ingredients.
3. Enter the correct settings (White, light crust & 2 lbs) and press the "Start" Button.
4. When the bread machine has finished baking the bread, unplug the bread machine.

5. Take out the bread pan and remove the bread from the bread pan. Place the bread on a cooling rack. Use oven mitts when removing the bread pan as it will be very hot!

6. Optional – right after you remove the hot bread from the bread pan and place it on the cooling rack, you can use a pastry brush to brush 1 tbsp of melted butter on the top of the bread. This creates a more golden crust and adds even more buttery flavor. This works best when the bread is still hot. Fyi – do not use too much melted butter or it will run all over the sides of the bread. Also do not brush on when the bread has cooled down.

7. Let the bread cool on the cooling rack for 1-2 hours before cutting.

Nutritional Value (Amount per Serving):

Calories: 197; Fat: 6.47; Carb: 29.76; Protein: 5.1

Sourdough Bread in a Bread Machine

Prep Time: 10 mins   Cook Time: 7 hours   Serves: 12

Ingredients:

- 1 1/4 cups water
- 1/4 cup unsalted butter melted
- 4 cups bread flour
- 2 tbsps granulated sugar
- 1/2 tbsp salt
- 1/2 cup sourdough starter bubbly and active

Directions:

1. Add the water and melted butter to the bread machine.
2. On top of that add the bread flour, sugar and salt.
3. Lastly, add the sourdough starter.
4. Use the dough function on the bread machine.
5. Optional: After the first knead cycle finishes, I press the button again and let it knead the dough one more time.
6. Next, I just allow the dough to sit in the bread machine for about 6 hours, or until the dough nearly rises to the top of the bread pan. I like to spritz the top with water a few times to make sure the dough doesn't dry out on top. (Optional, but also helps the crust to turn golden in the baking step.)
7. After the dough has risen for several hours, I go to the bake function and select the option for dark crust. This makes the bake time 1 hour.
8. Pull the bread out of the bread maker and allow to cool.

Nutritional Value (Amount per Serving):

Calories: 223; Fat: 3.94; Carb: 38.78; Protein: 8.86

Bread Machine Crusty Sourdough Bread

Prep Time: 10 mins   Cook Time: 3 hrs 30 mins   Serves: 12

Ingredients:

Sourdough Starter
- 1 1/2 tsps bread machine or quick active dry yeast
- 4 cups lukewarm water (105°F to 115°F)
- 3 cups All-Purpose Flour or Bread Flour
- 4 tsps sugar

Bread
- 1/2 cup water
- 3 cups Bread Flour
- 2 tbsps sugar
- 1 1/2 tsps salt
- 1 tsp bread machine or quick active dry yeast

Directions:

1. Make sourdough starter at least 1 week before making bread. In large glass bowl, dissolve 1 1/2 tsps yeast in warm water. Stir in 3 cups flour and 4 tsps sugar. Beat with electric mixer on medium speed about 1 minute or until smooth. Cover loosely; let stand at room temperature about 1 week or until mixture is bubbly and has a sour aroma. Transfer to 2-quart or larger nonmetal bowl. Cover tightly; refrigerate until ready to use.

2. Use sourdough starter once a week or stir in 1 tsp sugar. After using starter, replenish it by stirring in 3/4 cup all-purpose flour, 3/4 cup water and 1 tsp sugar until smooth. Cover loosely; let stand in warm place at least 1 day until bubbly. Cover tightly; refrigerate until ready to use. To use, stir cold starter; measure cold starter, and let stand until room temperature (starter will expand as it warms up).

3. Measure 1 cup of the sourdough starter and all remaining bread ingredients carefully, placing in bread machine pan in the order recommended by the manufacturer.

4. Select White. Use Medium or Light color. Do not use delay cycle. (Total time will vary with appliance and setting.) Remove baked bread from pan; cool on cooling rack.

Nutritional Value (Amount per Serving):

Calories: 287; Fat: 1.04; Carb: 60.1; Protein: 8.36

Bread Machine Potato Flake Sourdough Loaf

Prep Time: 8 hrs 20 mins   Cook Time: 2 hrs (varies)   Serves: 10

Ingredients:

- 1/2 cup active potato flake starter
- 1/3 cup warm water not hot, or it can kill your starter
- 2 tbsps oil vegetable oil or olive oil works well
- 2 cups bread flour
- 2 1/2 tbsps sugar
- 1 tsp salt

Directions:

1. Unplug the bread machine, remove the bread machine pan and add all of the wet ingredients (water, oil, active starter) into it.
2. After all of the wet ingredients are added, continue by adding the dry ingredients (bread flour, sugar, salt.)
3. Place it back into the bread machine. Select a cycle on the bread machine that will knead the dough for about 10 minutes.
4. After it is done kneading you can take the dough out and remove the paddle if you'd like. This will prevent you from having to remove it after it is done baking. Leaving it in is completely fine, but it will leave a hole in the bottom of your bread.
5. Turn off the bread machine and after the dough has risen for about 8 hours you can chose the bake setting. This bakes the bread with a medium darkness of crust.
6. After it has done baking, remove the insert, carefully with oven mitts, and allowed it to cool until I could handle it comfortably with my hands.
7. The bread should easily come out of the bread machine insert. Allow it to fully cool before slicing.

Nutritional Value (Amount per Serving):

Calories: 119; Fat: 0.54; Carb: 24.74; Protein: 3.44

Sourdough Sandwich Bread

Prep Time: 5 mins   Cook Time: 3 hrs 50 mins   Serves: 12

Ingredients:

- 1 cup sourdough starter
- 2/3 cup milk
- 2 tbsp butter cut into about 8 small cubes
- 3 cups bread flour
- 2 tbsp sugar
- 1 tbsp salt
- 1 1/2 tsp active dry yeast

Directions:

1. Place the milk, starter and then the butter cubes in the bread machine pan.
2. Evenly place the 3 cups of flour over the liquid ingredients.

3. Using a spoon, make three small wells in the flour and place the sugar, salt, and yeast each in one of the indentations.
4. Place in the bread machine and choose the white cycle.
5. When the machine beeps (mine takes 3 hours and 50 minutes) carefully pull out the pan (it's hot!) and remove the bread.
6. Let cool on a wire rack before slicing.

Nutritional Value (Amount per Serving):

Calories: 207; Fat: 3.43; Carb: 36.84; Protein: 6.79

Favorite Bread Machine Sourdough Loaf

Prep Time: 5 mins
Cook Time: 20 mins, plus 2-hr additional time
Serves: 12

Ingredients:

- 3 ½ cups all-purpose flour
- 2 tbsps sugar
- 2 tsps salt
- 2 ¼ tsps active dry yeast
- ¾ cup milk, warmed
- 1 ½ tbsps butter, softened
- 1 cup sourdough starter

Directions:

1. Add 1 cup flour, sugar, salt, and yeast to your bread pan. Run on the white bread cycle to stir these ingredients together. I use the dark crust setting for this recipe.
2. Slowly add warm milk and softened butter to dry mixture while the bread machine is still stirring. Then do the same with the sourdough starter.
3. Add the remaining 2-½ cups of flour slowly to the wet mixture. It may seem like too much flour, as the dough will get very crumbly, but it will all get kneaded into the bread. I've found that it helps to press down on the dough as the machine is still kneading to get it to pick up all of the bits of dough.
4. Close the top of the bread machine and let it finish out its cycle. When the bread is done baking, remove it from the pan immediately and let it cool on a rack to prevent it from getting soggy.

Nutritional Value (Amount per Serving):

Calories: 225; Fat: 2.98; Carb: 41.93; Protein: 7.49

Chapter 3: Fruit breads

Banana Bread - Quick Bread for Machines

Prep Time: 15 mins   Cook Time: 1 hr   Serves: 10

Ingredients:

- 2 bananas, peeled and halved lengthwise
- 2 cups all-purpose flour
- ¾ cup white sugar
- 2 large eggs
- 3 tbsps vegetable oil
- 1 tsp baking powder
- ½ tsp baking soda

Directions:

1. Place bananas, flour, sugar, eggs, oil, baking powder, and baking soda in the pan of the bread machine.
2. Select Dough setting; press start. Mix dough until well combined and bananas are mashed, 3 to 5 minutes. Use a rubber spatula to push dough from the sides of the bread pan if necessary. Press stop, then smooth out the top of the loaf with a rubber spatula.
3. Select Bake setting; press start. Bake in the bread machine until a toothpick inserted into the center comes out clean. If there is batter on the toothpick, reset the machine on Bake and continue baking for 10 to 15 minutes.
4. Remove the pan from the machine. Allow bread to remain in the pan for 10 minutes before transferring it to a wire rack to cool completely.

Nutritional Value (Amount per Serving):

Calories: 221; Fat: 8.55; Carb: 33.84; Protein: 4.11

Cranberry Orange Bread (for Bread Machine)

Prep Time: 5 mins   Cook Time: 3 hrs   Serves: 12

Ingredients:

- 3 cups all-purpose flour
- 1 cup dried cranberries
- ¾ cup plain yogurt
- ½ cup warm water
- 3 tbsps honey
- 1 tbsp butter, melted
- 2 tsps active dry yeast
- 1 ½ tsps salt
- 1 tsp orange oil

Directions:

1. Place flour, cranberries, yogurt, warm water, honey, melted butter, yeast, salt, and orange oil in the pan of a bread machine in the order recommended by the manufacturer.
2. Select "White" and "Light crust" Settings; press start.
3. Remove bread from pan, place on a cake rack, and allow to cool completely before slicing.

Nutritional Value (Amount per Serving):

Calories: 162; Fat: 1.97; Carb: 31.36; Protein: 4.74

Cranberry Orange Breakfast Bread

Prep Time: 5 mins   Cook Time: 3 hrs   Serves: 12

Ingredients:

- 1 ⅛ cups orange juice
- 2 tbsps vegetable oil
- 2 tbsps honey
- 3 cups bread flour
- 1 tbsp dry milk powder
- ½ tsp ground cinnamon
- ½ tsp ground allspice
- 1 tsp salt
- 1 (0.25 oz.) package active dry yeast
- 1 tbsp grated orange zest
- 1 cup sweetened dried cranberries
- ⅓ cup chopped walnuts

Directions:

1. Place ingredients in the pan of the bread machine in the order recommended by the manufacturer. Select White cycle; press start.
2. Add the cranberries and nuts at the signal, or about 5 minutes before the kneading cycle has finished.
3. Remove loaf from the machine after the cycle is done and allow it to cool before slicing.

Nutritional Value (Amount per Serving):

Calories: 196; Fat: 4.48; Carb: 34.14; Protein: 4.96

Bread Machine Cranberry Raisin Bread

Prep Time: 5 mins   Cook Time: 3 hrs   Serves: 12

Ingredients:

- 1 1/2 cups water (warm)
- 4 tbsps unsalted butter (sliced & softened)
- 3 cups bread flour
- 1 cup old fashioned oatmeal
- 1/3 cup light brown sugar

- 1 1/2 tsps salt
- 1 1/2 tsps bread machine yeast
- 4 tbsps dried cranberries
- 4 tbsps golden raisins

Directions:

1. Starting with the water, you should add all of the ingredients (except the cranberries & golden raisins) into the bread machine "bucket" (bread pan).
2. Enter the correct settings into the bread machine (2 lb, light crust and White) and press the start button.
3. After the bread machine has finished its first kneading cycle (and before the second kneading cycle), add the cranberries and golden raisins.
4. When the bread machine has finished baking the bread, unplug the bread machine. Remove the bread and place it on a cooling rack. Use oven mitts when removing the bread machine container (bread loaf pan) as it will be very hot!
5. After removing the bread, don't forget to remove the mixing paddle if it is stuck in the bread. Use oven mitts as the mixing paddle will be very hot coming out of the bread machine. Or wait until the bread is completely cooled and then remove the mixing paddle.

Nutritional Value (Amount per Serving):

Calories: 243; Fat: 6.64; Carb: 39.8; Protein: 5.71

Bread Machine Hawaiian Bread – Pineapple & Coconut

Prep Time: 15 mins   Cook Time: 3 hrs   Serves: 12

Ingredients:

- 1 1/4 cups pineapple juice (warm)– use canned pineapple juice. Do not use fresh pineapple juice. 4
- Tbsps unsalted butter (softened)
- 1 tsp vanilla extract
- 3 1/2 cups bread flour
- 1/2 cup sweetened coconut flakes (or shredded coconut) – packed cup.
- 4 tbsps light brown sugar (packed)
- 1 1/2 tsps salt
- 1 1/2 tsps bread machine yeast (or instant yeast)– not active dry yeast

Directions:

1. Soften the butter.
2. Add the pineapple juice, softened butter & vanilla extract into the bread

pan and then add the other ingredients. Place the instant yeast/bread machine yeast in last and the yeast should not touch the liquid (until the bread machine is turned on and the ingredients start to be mixed together by the bread machine).

3. Plug in the bread machine. Enter the correct settings (2 lb, light crust, White) and press the "Start" Button.

4. When the bread machine has finished baking the bread, unplug the bread machine and remove the bread pan from the bread machine. Wear oven mitts as the bread pan & bread machine will be hot.

5. Remove the bread from the bread pan and place the bread on a wire cooling rack. Use oven mitts when removing the bread as the bread & bread pan will be hot.

6. Optional – right after removing the bread from the bread pan (while the bread is still very hot), brush on 1 or 2 tbsps of melted butter on the top crust of the bread. This creates a more buttery top to the bread. Use a pastry brush to brush on the butter.

7. Let the bread cool on the wire cooling rack for 1-2 hours before cutting.

Nutritional Value (Amount per Serving):

Calories: 197; Fat: 2.81; Carb: 36.68; Protein: 5.95

Bread Machine Raisin Bread (Golden Raisins)

Prep Time: 5 mins   Cook Time: 3 hrs   Serves: 12

Ingredients:

- 1 1/2 cups milk (lukewarm)
- 4 tbsps butter (sliced & softened)
- 2 tsps molasses
- 3 cups bread flour
- 1 cup oatmeal – do not pre-moisten the flakes. Use dry flakes.
- 1/2 cup brown sugar (packed)
- 1 1/2 tsps salt
- 1 1/2 tsps bread machine yeast
- 1 cup raisins (golden raisins)

Directions:

1. Pour the milk into the bread pan and then add the other ingredients (except the golden raisins). Place the bread machine yeast in last and the yeast should not touch the liquid or salt (until the bread machine is turned on and the ingredients start to be mixed together). Fyi – do not place the salt where you plan to add the yeast.

2. Enter the correct settings into the bread machine (2 lb, light crust and

White) and press the start button.

3. After the bread machine has finished its first kneading cycle (and before it has started the second kneading cycle), add the golden raisins.

4. When the bread machine has finished baking the bread, unplug the bread machine. Remove the bread and place it on a cooling rack. Use oven mitts when removing the bread machine container (bread loaf pan) as it will be very hot!

5. After removing the bread, don't forget to remove the mixing paddle if it is stuck in the bread. Use oven mitts as the mixing paddle will be very hot coming out of the bread machine. Or wait until the bread is completely cooled and then remove the mixing paddle.

6. Before using your bread machine, you should read the bread machine manufacturer's instructions in order to use the bread machine effectively and safely.

Nutritional Value (Amount per Serving):

Calories: 254; Fat: 7.4; Carb: 41.13; Protein: 5.76

Pear Yeast Bread (Bread Machine)

Prep Time: 5 mins   Cook Time: 3 hrs   Serves: 12

Ingredients:

- 1 (15 oz.) can pear halves, undrained
- ½ tsp almond extract
- 2 tbsps butter or 2 tbsps margarine, softened
- 1 tbsp brown sugar
- 1 ½ tsps salt
- 1 tsp ground cinnamon
- ¼ tsp ground nutmeg
- 3 ½ cups bread flour
- 2 ¼ tsps active dry yeast

Directions:

1. In a blender or food processor, combine the pears and extract; cover and process until pureed. Pour into bread machine pan.

2. Add the remaining ingredients in order suggested by manufacturer. Select White setting. Choose desired crust color and loaf size.

3. Bake according to bread machine directions (check dough after 5 minutes of mixing; add 1 to 2 tbsps water or flour if needed).

Nutritional Value (Amount per Serving):

Calories: 160; Fat: 2.82; Carb: 28.41; Protein: 5.27

Bread Machine French Pear Bread

Prep Time: 10 mins   Cook Time: Varies according to different bread machines   Serves: 16

Ingredients:

- 1/4 cup warm water
- 3/4 cup mashed canned pears
- 1 tbsp honey
- 1 egg, beaten
- 3 cups bread flour
- 3/4 tsp salt
- 1/8 tsp black pepper
- 1 tsp bread machine yeast

Directions:

1. Place all the ingredients in the bread machine in the order directed by the machine manufacturer. Set on White, light crust settings.
2. When bread is baked, remove the pan from the machine.
3. Let cool for 5 minutes then remove the bread from the pan and let cool completely on a wire rack before slicing.
4. Store the bread in an airtight container at room temperature for up to 3 days.

Nutritional Value (Amount per Serving):

Calories: 115; Fat: 1.05; Carb: 22.26; Protein: 3.76

Strawberry Bread III

Prep Time: 10 mins   Cook Time: 45   Serves: 15

Ingredients:

- 1 (10 oz.) package frozen sweetened strawberries, thawed
- ½ cup vegetable oil
- 2 eggs
- 1 tsp baking soda
- ½ tsp baking powder
- ½ tsp ground cinnamon
- 1 cup white sugar
- 1 ½ cups all-purpose flour
- ½ cup chopped pecans

Directions:

1. Drain the strawberries, reserving 1/4 cup of the juice. In a large mixing bowl stir together the oil, eggs, baking soda, baking powder, cinnamon, sugar and flour. Fold in the pecans, strawberries and 1/4 cup of their juice.
2. Pour the mixture into your bread machine pan and place it in the machine. Select the Ultra Fast setting cycle and press start.

3. Remove pan from bread maker and let cool completely before removing bread from pan.

Nutritional Value (Amount per Serving):

Calories: 193; Fat: 13.65; Carb: 15.93; Protein: 3.28

Sweet Hawaiian Mango Yeast Bread (Bread Machine)

Prep Time: 5 mins   Cook Time: 3 hrs   Serves: 12

Ingredients:

- ¾ cup guava or 3/4 cup mango nectar
- 1 egg
- 2 tbsps melted butter
- 3 tbsps honey
- ¾ tsp salt
- 3 cups bread flour
- 2 tbsps dry milk
- 2 tsps fast rising yeast or 2 tsps quick-rising yeast
- 1 cup chopped dried mango (chopped to the size of raisins)

Directions:

1. Place ingredients in bread machine container in order directed by manufacturer.
2. Cycle: White.
3. Setting: Medium Crust.
4. Add mango at the beep (20 min after start).
5. For those of you who like a softer crust, as soon as it comes out of the bread machine, place in a plastic grocery bag and tie it closed till it cools.

Nutritional Value (Amount per Serving):

Calories: 216; Fat: 2.41; Carb: 40.71; Protein: 5.85

Bread Machine Banana Bread

Prep Time: 10 mins   Cook Time: 1 hr 40 mins   Serves: 12

Ingredients:

- 3 bananas (ripe & MEDIUM-sized bananas) – For the best results, you should use exactly 1 cup of mashed bananas.
- 8 tbsps unsalted butter (softened)
- 2 eggs (lightly beaten) – Use large eggs (not extra large or jumbo eggs)
- 1 tsp Vanilla Extract

- 1 cup light brown Sugar (packed cup)
- 2 cups flour (all-purpose)
- 1 tsp baking soda
- 1 tsp baking powder
- 1/2 tsp salt
- 1/2 cup chopped walnuts or mini chocolate chips (optional)
- 1 tsp ground cinnamon (optional) – Some people like to add cinnamon if their bananas are not super ripe.

Directions:

1. Beat the eggs.
2. Mash bananas with a fork.
3. Soften the butter in a microwave.
4. Add the mashed bananas, butter, eggs & vanilla extract into the bread pan and then add the other ingredients. Try to follow the order of the ingredients listed above so that liquid ingredients are placed in the bread pan first and the dry ingredients second. Be aware that the bread pan should be removed from the bread machine before you start to add any ingredients. This helps to avoid spilling any material inside the bread machine. The bread machine should always be unplugged when removing the bread pan.
5. Put the bread pan (with all of the ingredients) back into the bread machine, close the bread machine lid and then plug in the bread machine.
6. Enter the bread machine settings (Cake, Light Color, 2lb) and press the start button.
7. Optional – If you want to add chopped walnuts or mini chocolate chips to enhance this basic banana bread recipe, please add them after the first bread machine mixing cycle and before the second mixing (final mixing).
8. When the bread machine has finished baking the bread, unplug the bread machine, remove the bread pan and place it on a wooden cutting board. Use oven mitts when removing the bread pan because it will be very hot!
9. After removing the bread pan from the bread machine, you should let the banana bread stay within the warm bread pan on a wooden cutting board for 10 minutes (as this finishes the baking process) before you remove the banana bread from the bread pan. Wear oven mitts.
10. After the 10 minute "cooldown", you should remove the banana bread from the bread pan and place the banana bread on a wire cooling rack to finish cooling. Use oven mitts when removing the bread.
11. You should allow the banana bread to completely cool before cutting. This can take up to 2 hours. Otherwise, the banana bread will break (crumble) more easily when cut.

Nutritional Value (Amount per Serving):

Calories: 241; Fat: 8.96; Carb: 36.9; Protein: 4.25

Chapter 4: Gluten-free Breads

Low Carb Low Fat Gluten Free Bread

Prep Time: 10 mins   Cook Time: 3 hrs   Serves: 13

Ingredients:

- 1 cup water
- 2 tbsps water
- 2 large eggs
- 2 tbsps butter melted and cooled, (or oil)
- 1-1/2 cups superfine blanched almond flour Bob's Red Mill
- 2 tbsps superfine blanched almond flour
- 2/3 cup golden flax seed meal
- 1/2 cup brown rice protein or pea protein or both (or any bean flour)
- 2 tbsps psyllium husk powder
- 2 tsps instant dry yeast (SAF)
- 1/2 tsp salt
- 1/4 tsp monk fruit extract powder no sugar alcohol (Lakanto)
- 1-1/2 tsps guar gum - (optional) without, the bread is more fragile

Directions:

1. Add 1 cup plus 2 tbsps water, eggs, and cooled melted butter to the bowl of your bread maker.
2. In a separate bowl, whisk together the almond flour, flax seed meal, fava bean flour, yeast, and monk fruit extract powder; add to the liquid ingredients.
3. Transfer to the bowl of your bread machine and select the gluten-free function and light crust color.

Nutritional Value (Amount per Serving):

Calories: 159; Fat: 7.76; Carb: 16.28; Protein: 7.19

Paleo Bread Machine Recipe

Prep Time: 15 mins   Cook Time: 3 hours   Serves: 16

Ingredients:

- 4 tbsp Chia seeds
- 1 tbsp flax meal
- ¾ cup + 1 Tbsp water
- ¼ cup coconut oil
- 3 eggs (room temperature)
- ½ cup almond milk
- 1 tbsp maple syrup or honey
- 2 cups almond flour
- 1 ¼ cups tapioca flour
- ⅓ cup coconut flour
- 1 tsp Real Salt
- ¼ cups flax meal
- 1 tsp baking soda
- 2 tsp cream of tartar mixed well with:

- 2 tsp bread machine yeast

Directions:

1. Combine the Chia seeds and tbsp of flax meal in a bowl. Stir in the water and set aside. The mixture will thicken into a gel as it stands.
2. Melt the coconut oil and let it cool down to lukewarm. Whisk in the eggs, almond milk and maple syrup or honey.
3. Whisk in the Chia seed and flax meal gel. When it's well combined, pour it into the pan of the bread maker.
4. Stir the almond flour, tapioca flour, coconut flour, salt and ¼ cup of flax meal together.
5. Thoroughly mix the cream of tartar and baking soda. Add it to the other dry ingredients and stir well.
6. Pour the dry ingredients into the bread machine. Make a little well on top and add the yeast.
7. Start the machine on the Whole Wheat cycle for a 2 lb. loaf.

Nutritional Value (Amount per Serving):

Calories: 127; Fat: 6.59; Carb: 14.68; Protein: 2.7

Beautiful Gluten Free Bread Machine Recipe

Prep time: 15 mins   Cook time: 40 mins   Serves: 6

Ingredients:

- 1 cup Warm water
- 3 eggs
- 1 tsp. Cider Vinegar
- 2 tbs. oil (I use olive or avocado oil)
- 1 1/2 cups Almond Flour
- 1 1/2 cups Tapioca Flour
- 1 tbs. Active Dry Yeast
- 1 tsp. Xantham Gum
- 2 tsp. Sea Salt
- 1 tbs. Psyllium Husk

Directions:

1. Add the warm water, vinegar, oil, and eggs to the bread pan.
2. Lightly fill and level the almond flour and tapioca starch then add to the pan. Do not pack the flours into the measuring cup.
3. Add xantham gum, yeast, salt, and psyllium husk on top of the flours in the pan.
4. Select the gluten-free bake option.
5. While the bread machine is mixing, be sure to scrape the corners and edges.
6. Remove the loaf pan with an oven mitt, Invert the pan, shake out the loaf onto a plate or cutting board and allow to cool before slicing.
7. Store the bread in an air-tight container in the fridge if you plan to use it

up in a day or two. If not, store it in the freezer and remove what you need.

Nutritional Value (Amount per Serving):

Calories: 257; Fat: 9.67; Carb: 36.94; Protein: 5.54

Gluten-Free White Bread for Bread Machines

Prep Time: 5 mins   Cook Time: 1 hr   Serves: 12

Ingredients:

- 3 large eggs
- 1 tbsp cider vinegar
- ¼ cup olive oil
- ¼ cup honey
- 1 ½ cups buttermilk, at room temperature
- 1 tsp salt
- 1 tbsp xanthan gum
- ⅓ cup cornstarch
- ½ cup potato starch
- ½ cup soy flour
- 2 cups white rice flour
- 1 tbsp active dry yeast

Directions:

1. Place ingredients into a bread machine in the order listed, or follow the order recommended by the manufacturer if different.
2. Select the Gluten-Free cycle. Five minutes into the cycle, check the consistency of dough. Add additional rice flour or liquid if necessary.
3. Let bread cool for 10 to 15 minutes before removing from the pan.

Nutritional Value (Amount per Serving):

Calories: 224; Fat: 7.08; Carb: 35.41; Protein: 5.08

Gluten Free Bread Machine Brioche

Prep Time: 10 mins   Cook Time: 3 hrs   Serves: 12

Ingredients:

- 4.5 tsp dry active yeast
- 1 cup superfine brown rice flour
- 1 1/2 cup tapioca starch
- 1/3 cup cornstarch
- 1/2 cup potato starch
- 1/3 cup sugar
- 3 tsps xanthan gum
- 1 tbsp guar gum
- 1.5 tbsp salt
- 3/4 cup warm milk
- 6 large eggs
- 4 tbsps unsalted butter at room temperature

Directions:

1. Mix wet ingredients in pan.
2. Mix dry ingredients (other than yeast) separately, then place on top of wet

ingredients.

3. Add yeast on top.
4. Follow your machines instructions to run a Gluten-free cycle.
5. Cool the loaf completely before slicing.

Nutritional Value (Amount per Serving):

Calories: 234; Fat: 6.91; Carb: 39.28; Protein: 3.84

Gluten Free Cheddar Cheese Bread with Rice Flour

Prep Time: 10 mins   Cook Time: 4 hours   Serves: 14 slices

Ingredients:

Wet Ingredients
- 3 eggs
- 1 ½ cups water
- 2 tbsp. Vegetable oil

Dry Ingredients
- 2 ¼ tsp. Active dry yeast
- 2 cups white rice flour
- 1 cup brown rice flour
- ¼ cup dry milk powder for a dairy free option
- 2 tbsp. white sugar
- 1 tbsp. poppy seeds
- 1 ½ dried dill weed
- 3 ½ tsp. xanthan gum
- 1 tsp. salt
- 1 ½ cups shredded sharp Cheddar cheese try Daiya for a dairy free option

Directions:

1. In a medium bowl, combine the room temperature wet ingredients and mix well.
2. In a large bowl, mix together all the dry ingredients. Use a wire whisk to make sure it's all thoroughly mixed.
3. In the pan of your bread machine, add the wet ingredients first, then add the dry ingredients on top.
4. Select whole wheat setting and press start.
5. For the first 5 minutes or so, keep a spatula handy to push the mixture down and make sure it's mixing well.
6. After the setting is done, remove the beautiful, long awaited loaf from the pan and let it cool on a wire rack.

Nutritional Value (Amount per Serving):

Calories: 237; Fat: 7.67; Carb: 33.1; Protein: 8.55

Gluten Free Brown Rice Bread Bread Machine

Prep Time: 15 mins   Cook Time: 3 hrs 40 mins   Serves: 4

Ingredients:

- 1 1/2 cups filtered water
- 3 tbsps oil
- 3 tbsps honey
- 1 tsp of sea salt
- 1 tbsp xanthan gum
- 2 3/4 cups brown rice flour
- 3/4 cup tapioca flour
- 2 1/4 tsp Active Dry Yeast

Directions:

1. Add ingredients in the order listed. Sprinkle the yeast very evenly over the other ingredients.
2. For a quicker (but heavier) loaf, run the "dough" setting for 20-40 minutes, till the loaf has risen fairly well.
3. When the dough cycle is complete, manually change the bread maker to the bake setting. Total time in the bread maker will be about 2 1/3 hours, depending on how long you let it run in the dough cycle.
4. For a lighter loaf, run the bread maker on the whole wheat setting (this takes about 3 hours and 40 minutes).

Nutritional Value (Amount per Serving):

Calories: 642; Fat: 13.84; Carb: 120.78; Protein: 9.01

Easy Gluten Free White Rice Flour Bread for the Bread Machine

Prep Time: 10 mins   Cook Time: 2 hrs 44 mins   Serves: 12

Ingredients:

- 3 eggs room temperature
- 1 ½ cups water warmed to 70 – 80 degrees F
- 3 tbsps vegetable oil
- 1 tsp apple cider vinegar
- 2 ¼ cups white rice flour
- 1 cup tapioca starch
- 2 tsps xanthan gum
- 1 ½ tsp salt
- ½ cup dry coconut milk powder
- 3 tbsps white sugar
- 2 ¼ tsps active dry yeast

Directions:

1. In a medium size bowl or measuring cup, mix the eggs, water, oil and vinegar.
2. In a large bowl, add the rice flour, xanthan gum, salt, dry coconut milk powder and sugar. Mix with a whisk until incorporated.
3. Add the liquid to the bread machine pan, then add the flour mixture on top

the liquid.

4. Add the yeast in the very center - do not mix in.
5. Select the gluten free setting for a 2 lb loaf, and medium crust setting.
6. When the kneading cycle starts, scrape down the pan with a spatula and thoroughly mix the batter.
7. When the cycle is over, remove the pan and let the bread cool in the pan for 10 – 15 minutes on a wire rack.
8. Carefully remove from the pan and let it cool completely before cutting.

Nutritional Value (Amount per Serving):

Calories: 289; Fat: 6.6; Carb: 51.36; Protein: 6.17

Bread Machine Gluten Free Banana Bread

Prep Time: 10 mins   Cook Time: 1 hr 40 mins   Serve: 12

Ingredients:

- 1 1/4 cups bananas (ripe) – roughly 2 1/2 large bananas
- 8 tbsps unsalted butter (softened) – 115 grams
- 2 eggs (large)
- 2 cups gluten free all purpose flour – this recipe is based on using gluten free all purpose flour (not measure for measure flour) that includes xanthan gum. See the tips section for more information.
- 1 cup light brown sugar (packed cup)
- 1 tsp vanilla extract
- 1 tsp baking soda
- 1 tsp baking powder
- 1/2 tsp salt

Directions:

1. Lightly beat the eggs.
2. Mash bananas with a fork.
3. Soften the butter in your microwave.
4. Add the mashed bananas, butter and eggs into the bread pan and then add the other ingredients. Try to follow the order of the ingredients listed above so that liquid ingredients are placed in the bread pan first and the dry ingredients second.
5. Optional – consider premixing the ingredients in a large mixing bowl (versus allowing the bread machine to mix them) and then pouring the mixed batter into the bread pan. This helps to prevent flour from sticking to the sides of the bread pan.
6. Enter the bread machine settings (Cake, light color) and press the start button. The setting takes about 1 hr and 45 mins.

7. Optional – if you want to add chopped walnuts or mini chocolate chips to enhance your gluten free banana bread, please add them after the first bread machine mixing cycle and before the second mixing (final mixing).

8. When the bread machine has finished baking the bread, remove the bread pan and place it on a wooden cutting board. Use oven mitts when removing the bread pan because it will be very hot! And then let the banana bread stay within the warm bread pan on a wooden cutting board for 10 minutes before you remove the banana bread from the bread pan and place it on a wire cooling rack to finish cooling. Use oven mitts when removing the bread.

Nutritional Value (Amount per Serving):

Calories: 174; Fat: 10.89; Carb: 17.77; Protein: 2.02

Gluten-Free Linseed Brown Bread

Prep Time: 10 mins   Cook Time: 3 hrs   Serves: 12

Ingredients:

- 1 large egg
- 1 1/2 cups water
- 3tbsp dry milk powder
- 1 tsp lemon juice
- 3 tbsp sunflower oil
- 1 tbsp black treacle
- 2 tsp light brown sugar
- 1 tbsp gluten-free baking powder
- 1 3/4 cups brown rice flour
- 1/2 cup quinoa flour
- 1/2 cup buckwheat flour
- 1 tsbp xanthum gum
- 1½ tsp salt
- 1 tbsp linseed
- 1 tbsp active dried yeast

Directions:

1. Put your egg, milk powder and water to a bowl and take a whisk to them, building up a smooth paste, then drop this into the pan of your breadmaker.

2. Apply the lemon juice, sugar, treacle and oil. Then add the flour, gum, linseed and salt to the top, and finally, sprinkle your yeast over all of these ingredients.

3. Start your bread machine to bake on the White setting for 1.5lb loaf,

providing a dark crust if this is an option open to you. Leave the breadmaker to do what it does best.

4. When complete, leave the loaf to cool for a minimum of 10 minutes on an appropriate rack and enjoy!

Nutritional Value (Amount per Serving):

Calories: 187; Fat: 5.37; Carb: 31.15; Protein: 4.39

Gluten-Free Corn Bread

Prep Time: 10 mins   Cook Time: 2 hrs   Serves: 12

Ingredients:

- 3 large eggs
- 1 cup milk
- 2 tsp lemon juice
- 3/4 cups melted white vegetable fat
- 2 1/4 maize flour
- 1½tsp salt
- 1tbsp gluten-free baking powder

Directions:

1. Crack your eggs into a bowl, and add the milk and lemon juice. Take your whisk to these ingredients and, once they've had a good mix, pour into the pan of your breadmaker.

2. Pour the remaining ingredients on top of your existing mix, and start your breadmaker on a Dough cycle.

3. Leave the machine for around five minutes, then lift the lid and take a flat implement to the sides to avoid sticking and ensure the contents are nice and smooth. Never use your fingers for this – it's what a spatula is for. You should probably do this twice, to be on the safe side.

4. Return the pan to the bread machine, and this time set the device to Bake, (depending on the make of your machine. This should take less than an hour, but feel free to keep an eye on the loaf within; if it has risen sufficiently and is smooth to the touch, it may be ready to come out).

5. Leave the corn bread on a cooling rack once it has completed its cycle, chop up into squares or slices that will fit onto a side plate, and serve to your hungry diners!

Nutritional Value (Amount per Serving):

Calories: 51; Fat: 2.91; Carb: 4.12; Protein: 2.53

Gluten Free Pear Cake Bread Recipe

Prep Time: 15 mins   Cook Time: 4 hrs   Serves: 12

Ingredients:

- 3 eggs
- 2 tsps of vanilla extract
- 1 tsp of salt
- 1 tbsp of ground cinnamon
- ¾ cup vegetable oil
- 2 cups of peeled and shredded pears
- 2 cups of white sugar
- 3 cups of gluten free all-purpose flour
- ¼ tsp of baking soda
- 1 tsp of baking powder

Additions:

1. 1 cup of chopped pecans but reserve until after the beep for addition of nuts or put into a fruit and nut hopper if you have one.
2. 1 peeled and thinly slice pear for topping

Directions:

1. Add the ingredients to the bread pan in the order indicated in the recipe and select the Gluten-free setting, 2 lb and medium crust. If you've reduced the ingredients to accommodate the settings on your machine, adjust accordingly.
2. When the machine beeps for addition of nuts, add the pecans to the dough mixture. When the bread has risen in the machine, top with the thin pear slices and quickly close the lid.
3. When done, let the loaf rest for 10 minutes and then remove from the pan and let cool on a wire rack.

Nutritional Value (Amount per Serving):

Calories: 451; Fat: 30.04; Carb: 38.96; Protein: 8.08

Perfect Bread Machine Gluten Free Bread

Prep Time: 5 mins   Cook Time: 2 hrs 25 mins   Serves: 12

Ingredients:

- 1 1/4 cup water
- 1/4 cup oil or 4 tbsp dairy free butter
- 3 eggs
- 1 1/4 tsp salt

- 3 tbsp honey or sugar
- 3 1/4 cup bob's red mill gluten-free 1-to-1 baking flour
- 2 tsp active dry yeast

Directions:

1. Add all ingredients, in the order listed, into the bread machine loaf pan (make sure kneading paddle is in the pan).
2. Place pan in bread machine and select Gluten-free program, then start. After 3-5 minutes of kneading, gently scrape down the dry ingredients stuck on the sides of the pan with a spatula.
3. The bread machine will take care of the rest including the rise and baking. It will beep when done, about 2 hours 15 minutes from the start.

Nutritional Value (Amount per Serving):

Calories: 271; Fat: 10.61; Carb: 36.29; Protein: 7.4

Gluten Free Banoffee Loaf (Bread Machine)

Prep Time: 10 mins   Cook Time: 3 hrs   Serves: 12

Ingredients:

- 1 packet of gluten free white/brown bread mix
- 4 small bananas - mashed
- 1 cup water
- 1 tsp cinnamon
- 1/2 chocolate chips - ideally chocolate chips from the baking aisle so they keep their shape at high temperatures
- 2/3 cup fudge pieces - ideally from the baking aisle too
- 3 tbsp sunflower oil
- 4 tbsp of toffee/biscuit/chocolate spread - anything to your taste!

Directions:

1. Make sure the bread maker pan has the kneading blade inserted.
2. Peel your bananas and mash until really smooth.
3. Add the water, oil and mashed bananas to the bread tin.
4. Add the flour on top of that.
5. Sprinkle the cinnamon, choc chips and fudge pieces over the top of the flour.
6. Set the bread maker to Gluten-free, dark crust.
7. Press the "start" Button and leave the machine to complete the "rest" And "knead" Cycles. As soon as they are complete, carefully scrape around the outside of the bread pan to bring any excess flour/choc chips that are sitting on the sides into the middle of the loaf. (use a soft spatula so you do not damage the pan).

8. Take 1 tbsp of spread and spoon onto the bread. Use the spoon to swirl it right into the middle of the loaf.
9. Repeat for the other 3 tbsp, all in different locations so you get swirls the whole way through the loaf.
10. Scatter the remaining choc chips and fudge pieces over the top of the loaf. Place the lid back down and let the bread complete the baking process!
11. Once the bake is done, carefully remove the bread pan from the bread maker and set aside for 5 mins to cool.
12. Then, tip the bread pan upside down to release the loaf. You may need to shake it/ tap it lightly on the surface to release the bread.
13. Place onto a cooling rack and leave for a minimum of 1 hour to cool completely before slicing.

Nutritional Value (Amount per Serving):

Calories: 418; Fat: 6.05; Carb: 93.13; Protein: 2.68

Gluten-Free Zucchini Bread Recipe (for Bread Machine)

Prep Time: 10 mins   Cook Time: 2 hrs   Serves: 10

Ingredients:

- 1/3 cup oil
- 3/4 cup zucchini, shredded
- 2 eggs
- 1/3 cup packed brown sugar
- 3 tbsp granulated sugar
- 1 1/2 cup gluten free featherlite flour

- 3/4 tsp cinnamon
- 1/4 tsp allspice
- 3/4 tsp salt
- 1/2 tsp baking soda
- 1/2 tsp baking powder
- 1/3 cup walnuts (optional)
- 1/3 cup raisins (optional)

Directions:

1. Place all ingredients in order listed into the bread machine pan.
2. Select Gluten-free.
3. Cool the loaf completely after the baking is done.
4. Enjoy!

Nutritional Value (Amount per Serving):

Calories: 161; Fat: 10.95; Carb: 14.14; Protein: 2.59

Gluten Free Garlic/Parmesan Bread Machine Recipe

Prep Time: 20 mins   Cook Time: 4 hrs   Serves: 12

Ingredients:

- 1 cup of room temperature water
- 1 large egg; lightly beaten
- 2 tbsps of softened raw butter
- 3 cups of all purpose gluten free flour
- 1/2 cups grated parmesan cheese
- 2 tbsps of sugar
- 2 tsps dried onion flakes
- 1 1/2 tsps garlic salt
- 2 1/2 tsps active dry yeast

Directions:

1. In your bread machine; add all wet ingredients, water, eggs, and butter. Next, add your dry ingredients flour, parmesan cheese, sugar, onion flakes, garlic powder.
2. Most importantly, make a small, hallow hole on top of your ingredients and fill with the yeast.
3. Furthermore, when preparing your gluten free garlic/parmesan bread machine it is essential to add your yeast last.
4. Close the lid, press Gluten-free cycle with light crust setting.
5. Throughout, the bread machine cycle all your ingredients will kneed, rise and then bake.
6. Once the cycle is complete remove bread immediately and let cool on a wire rack for about thirty minutes.
7. Slice desire thickness with a serrated bread knife. Serve bread warm with butter or plain.

Nutritional Value (Amount per Serving):

Calories: 196; Fat: 4.13; Carb: 33.3; Protein: 6.88

Gluten-Free Bread Machine Panettone

Prep Time: 1 hr 15 mins   Cook Time: 4 hrs   Serves: 12

Ingredients:

For the sponge:
- ¾ cups gluten-free flour
- 1 tsp instant dry yeast
- 2 tsps granulated sugar
- 1/2 cup plus 2 tbsps lukewarm water

For the dough:
- 2 large eggs
- 2 large egg yolks
- 2 tbsps water
- 1 tbsp honey
- 6 tbsps unsalted butter, softened
- 1 tsp pure vanilla extract

- 2 cups gluten-free flour
- 2 tbsps nonfat powdered milk
- 1/4 cup granulated sugar
- 1 tsp fine sea salt
- 1 tsp instant dry yeast
- ¾ to 1 cups golden raisins (see step 3 below)
- 1/8 cup candied orange peel, diced (optional)

Directions:

1. Combine the ingredients for the sponge in a medium glass bowl until well mixed. Cover with plastic wrap and set aside for one hour.
2. Meanwhile, measure out the 2 cups of flour, powdered milk, sugar, and salt for the dough into another bowl and stir well. Set aside.
3. Pick over the raisins, separating any that are clumped together and removing any attached stems. If you are including the candied orange peel, use only ¾ cup raisins; if not, use a full cup. After one hour, the sponge will have risen significantly. Now you can mix the dough in the machine.
4. Add the eggs, egg yolks, water, honey, vanilla, and all of the sponge to the pan in the bread machine. Cut the softened butter into 5 or 6 pieces and add it to the pan. Then add the reserved dry ingredients. Add the tsp of yeast last.
5. Select "Sweet" Mode and "medium" Crust setting with a loaf size of 2 lb. Use a spatula to scrape unmixed flour into the dough until you don't see any more dry bits on the bottom and in the corners. You may need to add another tbsp of water or so to get a moist, dough-like consistency as opposed to a dense, tough paste.
6. When the machine completes the first mixing cycle, add the raisins and candied orange peel now.
7. Once the machine has completed the second mixing cycle, use a plastic spatula coated with canola oil to even out the dough in the pan and smooth the top.
8. When the bread is completely baked, it will be tall and nicely browned. Carefully remove the pan from the machine, slide the loaf out of the pan, and let it cool completely on a wire rack before cutting. Enjoy toasted with butter and honey, or use it for some super-delicious french toast.

Nutritional Value (Amount per Serving):

Calories: 114; Fat: 5.86; Carb: 13.64; Protein: 1.96

Bread Machine Grain-Free Cassava Century Bread

Prep Time: 20 mins   Cook Time: 3 hrs 30 mins   Serves: 10

Ingredients:

Wet Ingredients:
- 3 eggs
- 1 tsp apple cider vinegar
- 1/2 cup melted ghee, butter, or coconut oil
- 1 tbsp honey, molasses, or maple syrup
- 1 1/2 cups warm almond or coconut milk (very warm to the wrist)

Dry Ingredients:
- 1 1/2 cup cassava flour
- 1/2 cup potato starch
- 1/2 cup arrowroot or tapioca starch
- 1/4 cup flax seed meal
- 1/1/2 tsp psyllium husk or 1 tsp of psyllium powder
- 1-2 tsp Himalayan salt (I use 2)
- 2 tsp rapid rise bread machine yeast

Directions:

1. Ensure all ingredients are room temperature and the almond or coconut milk is very warm. Mix the Wet Ingredients in a small bowl and whisk until well blended. Set this aside while you combine the Dry Ingredients together.
2. Set the Active Dry Yeast aside.
3. In a medium bowl, sift the cassava flour, starches, and salt into a medium bowl.
4. Whisk in the flax seed meal and the seeds making sure it is well combined.
5. Place the warm Wet Ingredients into the bread machine pan.
6. Pour the sifted and whisked Dry Ingredients over the wet mixture.
7. Make a hole with your finger and sprinkle in the Active Dry Yeast.
8. Use the Gluten-Free setting.

Nutritional Value (Amount per Serving):

Calories: 307; Fat: 22.53; Carb: 20.98; Protein: 7.33

Simple and Delicious Gluten Free Bread Machine Recipe

Prep Time: 5 mins   Cook Time: 4 hrs 15 mins   Serves: 12

Ingredients:

- 1½ cups water or milk warmed to 115 degrees F
- ¼ cup olive oil
- 2 eggs large
- ⅛ cup pure honey preferably local organic honey
- ¾ tsp apple cider vinegar

- 1 tsp salt
- 2½ cups gluten-free flour blend
- 1 tsp baking powder
- ½ tsp gelatin
- 2 tsp xanthan gum use only if flour blend does not contain
- 2¼ tsp active, instant, or bread machine yeast

Directions:

1. Add the ingredients in the order listed to the bread maker pan. The ingredients are listed in the order that Cuisinart machines require them to go.
2. Select the gluten-free bread setting. Choose the 1.5 lb loaf size and your preferred crust color. During the first kneading cycle, frequently check on the dough. If it's too dry, add more warm liquid 1 tbsp at a time until it begins to form a thick batter-like consistency roughly in the shape of ball. When the rising cycle completes, brush the dough with milk or an egg wash for a darker top.
3. When baking is complete, turn off the bread machine. Remove the bread pan using oven mitts and wait 10 minutes before carefully removing the bread. Cool on a wire rack completely before slicing.

Nutritional Value (Amount per Serving):

Calories: 116; Fat: 5.71; Carb: 14.35; Protein: 2.55

Best Whole Grain Gluten-Free Bread for a Bread Machine

Prep Time: 10 mins   Cook Time: 50 mins, plus 2-hr additional time   Serves: 10

Ingredients:

- 1 cup cornstarch
- ½ cup millet flour
- ½ cup tapioca starch
- ¼ cup sweet rice flour
- ¼ cup teff flour
- ¼ cup ground flax
- 2 tbsps psyllium husk
- 2 ½ tsps guar gum

- 2 large eggs
- 1 ⅔ cups warm water
- 3 tbsps canola oil
- 1 tsp white vinegar
- 2 ¾ tsps active dry yeast
- 1 ½ tsps salt
- ½ cup milk powder
- 3 tbsps white sugar

Directions:

1. Mix cornstarch, millet flour, tapioca flour, rice flour, teff flour, ground flax, psyllium husk, and guar gum in a bowl.
2. Place eggs, warm water, canola oil, vinegar, sugar, yeast, cornstarch mixture, salt, and milk in a bread machine pan in the order listed, or in the order listed by the manufacturer. Stir gently with a wooden spoon to

combine yeast with the rest of the ingredients.

3. Run "ultra-fast" cycle and select "dark" crust setting.

Nutritional Value (Amount per Serving):

Calories: 250; Fat: 2.64; Carb: 50.75; Protein: 6.24

Alison's Gluten-Free Bread

Prep Time: 15 mins   Cook Time: 2 hrs (varies)   Serves: 12

Ingredients:

- 1 egg
- ⅓ cup egg whites
- 1 tbsp apple cider vinegar
- ¼ cup canola oil
- ¼ cup honey
- 1 ½ cups warm skim milk
- 1 tsp salt
- 1 tbsp active dry yeast

- 1 tbsp xanthan gum
- ½ cup tapioca flour
- ¼ cup garbanzo bean flour
- ¼ cup millet flour
- 1 cup white rice flour
- 1 cup brown rice flour

Directions:

1. Place ingredients in the pan of the bread machine in the order recommended by the manufacturer. Select gluten-free cycle; press Start. Five minutes into the cycle, check the consistency of the dough. Add additional rice flour or liquid if necessary.
2. When bread is finished, let cool for 10 to 15 minutes before removing from pan.

Nutritional Value (Amount per Serving):

Calories: 270; Fat: 8.8; Carb: 39.75; Protein: 8.36

The Best Gluten Free Bread

Prep Time: 10 mins   Cook Time: 2 hrs 30 mins   Serves: 10

Ingredients:

Wet Ingredients
- 1.5 Cups Water
- 1/4 Cup Ghee (ghee is a clarified butter but you can opt for any oil that you like)
- 1.4 Cup Honey
- 1 tsp Apple Cider Vinegar
- 3 Eggs

Dry Ingredients
- 2 Cups Namaste Gluten Free Perfect Flour Blend

- 1/2 Cup Almond Flour
- 1/2 Cup Tapioca Flour
- 1.5 tsps Xanthan Gum
- 1 tsp Salt
- 2 tsps Dry Active Yeast

Directions:

1. To begin this bread, warm up the 1.5 Cups Water on the stovetop. You want the water just a little warm, not hot, just warm for the yeast to work. Then, add the remaining wet ingredients in the order that they are listed: 1/4 Cup Ghee, 1/4 Cup Honey, 1 tsp Apple Cider Vinegar. Mix these together really well. Add your 3 mixed Eggs and stir all wet ingredients together. Pour the wet ingredients in to your bread machine bowl.
2. Then add all the dry ingredients except for the yeast on top of the wet ingredients: 2 Cups Namaste Gluten Free Flour, 1/2 Cup Almond Flour, 1/2 Cup Tapioca Flour, 1.5 tsps Salt, 1.5 tsps Xanthan Gum.
3. Make a little well or nest in the middle of your dough. In this nest, put your 2 tsps Active Dry Yeast. Do not mix this in, just leave it in the nest.
4. Set your bread machine to the gluten-free setting and let it bake. Once it's done, let it cool before slicing. Enjoy!

Nutritional Value (Amount per Serving):

Calories: 298; Fat: 8.5; Carb: 53.99; Protein: 5.26

Low Carb Almond Bread Machine Bread

Prep Time: 15 mins   Cook Time: 3 hrs 45 mins   Serves: 12

Ingredients:

- 1 cup water
- 1 1⁄2 tbsps butter
- 1 tsp salt
- 2 tbsps almond milk
- 1 cup almond flour
- 1 cup soy flour
- 1 cup gluten-free flour
- 2 tbsps artificial sweetener
- 2 tsps bread machine yeast

Directions:

1. Place room temperature water and wet ingredients into bread machine.
2. Add flour and dry ingredients on top (if you are doing a delayed start, place yeast on top of the flour.)
3. Use 2 tbs sugar (will be consumed by the yeast), alternatively, 2 tbs of splenda.
4. Bake bread using white cycle, 1.5 lb loaf, medium crust.

Nutritional Value (Amount per Serving):

Calories: 66; Fat: 3.05; Carb: 7.06; Protein: 3.23

Chapter 5: Spice And Nut Breads

Bread Machine Apple Bread (with Nuts)

Prep Time: 10 mins   Cook Time: 1 hr 40 mins   Serves: 12

Ingredients:

- 1 cup applesauce (chunky-style)
- 1/4 cup vegetable oil (use a neutral flavored oil such as canola oil)
- 2 eggs
- 2 cups flour (all-purpose flour)
- 1/2 cup white granulated sugar
- 1/2 cup light brown sugar (packed cup)
- 1 tsp vanilla extract
- 1 tsp baking powder
- 1 tsp baking soda
- 1/2 tsp ground cinnamon
- 1/2 tsp salt
- 1 cup chopped walnuts

Directions:

1. Lightly beat the eggs.
2. Add the applesauce, vegetable oil, eggs and then the rest of the ingredients (except the chopped walnuts) into the bread pan.
3. Enter the bread machine settings (Cake, light crust) and press the start button.
4. After the first mixing cycle by your bread machine and before the second/ final mixing, add the chopped walnuts.
5. When the bake is finished, remove the bread pan and place the bread pan on a wooden cutting board. Let the bread stay within the bread pan for 10 minutes before you remove it from the bread pan. Use oven mitts when removing the bread pan because it will be very hot!
6. After removing the quick bread from the bread pan, place the bread on a cooling rack. Use oven mitts when removing the bread. Let the quick bread cool down for 60+ minutes or it will be more likely to break/crumble when cut into slices.
7. Don't forget to remove the mixing paddle if it is stuck in the bread. Use oven mitts as the mixing paddle could be hot.

Nutritional Value (Amount per Serving):

Calories: 214; Fat: 12.54; Carb: 21.26; Protein: 5.05

Bread Machine Cranberry Bread with Chopped Walnuts

Prep Time: 10 mins   Cook Time: 2 hrs 53 mins   Serves: 12

Ingredients:

- 1 1/8 cups milk (lukewarm)
- 4 tbsps unsalted butter (softened)
- 3 cups bread flour
- 2 tbsps light brown sugar
- 1 tsp salt
- 1 tsp bread machine yeast
- 1/2 cup chopped walnuts
- 1/2 cup dried cranberries

Directions:

1. Add the milk & softened butter into the bread pan and then add the other ingredients (except the dried cranberries & chopped walnuts – they are added later).
2. Place the bread machine yeast in last and the yeast should not touch the liquid or salt (until the bread machine is turned on and the ingredients start to be mixed together). Some people like to make a small "divot" on top of the flour in order to hold the yeast in one spot before the machine starts.
3. Enter the correct settings (1.5 lb, light crust & White) and press the "start" Button.
4. When the bread machine's first mixing cycle has stopped and before the second (& final) mixing cycle starts, you should add the dried cranberries & chopped walnuts. Fyi – see your bread machine manual on when & how to add fruits & nuts when using your bread machine. Always follow the manufacturer instructions for your specific bread machine.
5. When the bread machine has finished baking the bread, remove the bread pan from the unplugged bread machine. Use oven mitts when removing the bread machine container (bread pan) as it will be very hot!
6. Take the bread out of the bread pan and place the bread on a wire cooling rack. Wear oven mitts.
7. After removing the bread, don't forget to remove the mixing paddle if it is stuck in the bread. Use oven mitts as the mixing paddle will be very hot coming out of the bread machine. Or wait until the bread is completely cooled and then remove the mixing paddle.

Nutritional Value (Amount per Serving):

Calories: 194; Fat: 6.29; Carb: 28.43; Protein: 5.7

Oat Nut Bread

Prep Time: 2 hrs 45 mins   Cook Time: 40 mins   Serves: 12

Ingredients:

- 1 1/8 cups milk (warm) – fyi – 1 1/8 cups is equal to 1 cup plus 2 tbsps of milk.
- 4 tbsps unsalted butter (sliced & softened)
- 2 1/2 cups bread flour
- 3/4 cup oat flakes (oatmeal) – do not pre-moisten the oat flakes. I like to use plain old-fashioned oat flakes (oatmeal) to make this bread.
- 1/3 cup light brown sugar (packed cup)
- 1 1/2 tsps salt
- 1 1/2 tsps instant yeast (or bread machine yeast)
- 1 cup chopped walnuts

Directions:

1. Pour the milk & softened butter into the bread pan and then add the other ingredients. Place the instant yeast/bread machine yeast in last and the yeast should not touch the liquid (until the bread machine is turned on and the ingredients start to be mixed together by the bread machine). Fyi – many bakers like to make a crater/pocket in the top of the flour to hold the yeast so the yeast does not contact the liquid or salt in the bread pan.
2. Enter the correct settings (2 lb, light crust, White) and press the "Start" Button.
3. Add the chopped walnuts to the bread pan about 10 minutes after the start button was pressed. Fyi – you will be adding the chopped nuts during the dough "Rest" Period between the first and second mixing/kneading cycles.
4. When the bread machine has finished baking the bread, unplug the bread machine and remove the bread pan from the bread machine. Wear oven mitts as the bread pan & bread machine will be hot.
5. Remove the bread from the bread pan and place the bread on a cooling rack. Use oven mitts when removing the bread as the bread & bread pan will be hot.
6. After removing the bread, don't forget to remove the mixing paddle if it is stuck in the bread. Use oven mitts as the mixing paddle will be very hot coming out of the bread machine. Or wait until the bread is completely cooled and then remove the mixing paddle.
7. Let the bread cool on the cooling rack for 1-2 hours before cutting.

Nutritional Value (Amount per Serving):

Calories: 199; Fat: 8.03; Carb: 27.4; Protein: 6.9

The Absolute Best Bread Machine Banana Nut Bread

Prep Time: 15 mins   Cook Time: 1 hr 50 mins   Serves: 12

Ingredients:

- 3 beaten eggs
- 1 cup mashed bananas
- 2 cups all purpose flour
- 1 tbsp baking powder
- 1 tsp baking soda
- 1/2 cup melted butter
- 1/2 cup packed light brown sugar
- 1/2 tsp salt
- 1 tbsp vanilla extract
- 1/4 tsp ground mace
- 1/4 tsp ground allspice
- 3/4 cup chopped nuts (pecans, walnuts, almonds, etc.), optional

Directions:

1. In pan from bread machine, add all ingredients in the order listed except the nuts.
2. Place pan in bread machine, choose "cake" cycle and "light" crust.
3. When machine beeps for add-ins, sprinkle in nuts, scrape down the sides well with a rubber spatula, and return to baking.
4. When cycle is finished, allow bread to cool for ten minutes and then turn out on a cooling rack to cool completely.
5. Wrap bread tightly and store.

Nutritional Value (Amount per Serving):

Calories: 257; Fat: 15.12; Carb: 25.75; Protein: 5.49

Chocolate Walnut Bread Machine Bread

Prep Time: 15 mins   Cook Time: 45 mins   Serves: 12

Ingredients:

- 1 1/4 cups water
- 1 1/2 tsps vanilla extract
- 1 1/2 tsps table salt
- 3 tbsps granulated sugar
- 3 1/2 cups all-purpose flour
- 1 1/2 tsps instant yeast
- 3/4 cup walnut halves, toasted
- 3/4 cup semisweet chocolate chips

Directions:

1. Measure your flour by gently spooning it into a cup, then sweeping off any excess. Place all of the ingredients except the walnuts and chocolate chips into the pan of your bread machine. Program the machine for white.
2. Check the dough after 10 to 15 minutes of kneading; it should have formed a smooth ball, soft but not sticky. If necessary, adjust the dough's

consistency with additional water or flour.

3. Add the chips and nuts at the signal; or add them about 3 minutes before the end of the second kneading cycle.
4. When the baking cycle is complete, remove the pan from the machine and transfer the loaf to a rack to cool completely before slicing.
5. Store the bread for up to five days, well-wrapped at room temperature, or freeze for up to three months.

Nutritional Value (Amount per Serving):

Calories: 240; Fat: 6.88; Carb: 39.54; Protein: 5.41

Honey Walnut Bread

Prep Time: 5 mins   Cook Time: 4 hrs   Serves: 20

Ingredients:

- 1 1/2 cups hot water
- 5 tbsp. honey
- 3 tbsp. walnut oil
- 4 cups bread flour NOT all-purpose flour
- 1/3 cup nonfat dry milk powder
- 1 tsp. sea salt
- 1 1/4 tsp. bread machine yeast
- 1 cup walnuts very finely chopped (measure after chopping)

Directions:

1. Layer ingredients in order given in bread canister.
2. Place on white setting.
3. Allow bread to cool about 15 minutes before removing from oven.
4. Remove bread from canister and butter the top and sides with butter to prevent the crust from hardening.
5. Slice down when cool.

Nutritional Value (Amount per Serving):

Calories: 154; Fat: 4.91; Carb: 24.31; Protein: 3.42

Bread Machine Pumpkin Spice Quick Bread

Prep Time: 10 mins   Cook Time: 3 hrs 10 mins   Serves: 12

Ingredients:

- 1 cup sugar
- 1 cup canned pumpkin
- 1/3 cup vegetable oil
- 1 tsp vanilla

- 2 eggs
- 1 1/2 cups all-purpose flour
- 2 tsps baking powder
- 1/4 tsp salt
- 1 tsp ground cinnamon
- 1/4 tsp ground nutmeg
- 1/8 tsp ground cloves
- 1/2 cup chopped nuts, if desired

Directions:

1. Grease bread machine pan and kneading blade generously with shortening.
2. Measure carefully, placing all ingredients in bread machine pan in the order recommended by the manufacturer.
3. Select ultra-fast cycle only. After 3 minutes into cycle, open lid and carefully scrape down sides of pan. Close lid to continue with cycle.
4. Cool baked bread 10 minutes. Remove from pan to wire rack, or follow manufacturer's recommendation.

Nutritional Value (Amount per Serving):

Calories: 263; Fat: 16.84; Carb: 23.98; Protein: 6.52

Gingered Spice Bread

Prep Time: 15 mins   Cook time: 3 hrs 15 mins   Serves: 16

Ingredients:

- ¾ cup milk
- 3 tbsps molasses
- 1 large egg
- 2 tbsps butter or 2 tbsps margarine, cut up
- ¾ tsp salt
- 3 cups bread flour
- 1 tsp ground ginger
- ½ tsp ground cinnamon
- ¼ tsp ground cloves
- 2 tsps bread machine yeast

Directions:

1. Add ingredients to bread machine pan in the order suggested by manufacturer.
2. Select white bread cycle; light or medium color setting.
3. (If dough is too dry or stiff or too soft or slack, adjust dough consistency) Checking Dough Consistency: Check dough after 5 minutes of mixing; it should form a soft, smooth ball around the blade.
4. If dough is too stiff or dry, add additional liquid, 1 tsp at a time, until dough is of the right consistency.
5. If dough is too soft or sticky, add additional bread flour, 1 tsp at a time.

Nutritional Value (Amount per Serving):

Calories: 149; Fat: 3.69; Carb: 23.42; Protein: 5.19

Chapter 6: Vegetable Breads

Bread Machine Garlic Bread

Prep Time: 10 mins
Additional Time: 2 hrs 30 mins

Cook Time: 30 mins
Serves: 12

Ingredients:

- 1 cup warm water (110 degrees f)
- 1 tbsp butter
- 1 tbsp dry milk powder
- 1 tbsp white sugar
- 1 ½ tsps salt
- 1 ½ tbsps dried parsley
- 2 tsps garlic powder
- 3 cups bread flour
- 2 tsps active dry yeast

Directions:

1. Place ingredients mentioned above in the pan of the bread machine in the order recommended by the manufacturer.
2. Select the White cycle; press start.
3. Remove the bread from the machine with oven mitts after the cycle is done, and allow it to cool before slicing.

Nutritional Value (Amount per Serving):

Calories: 157; Fat: 1.87; Carb: 29.28; Protein: 6.13

Crusty Potato Bread

Prep Time: 5 mins   Cook Time: 3 hrs   Serves: 15

Ingredients:

- 3 ¼ cups bread flour
- ½ cup instant mashed potato flakes
- 1 tbsp white sugar
- 1 ½ tsps salt
- 2 tbsps butter
- 1 ¼ cups water
- 2 tsps instant yeast

Directions:

1. Place ingredients in the pan of the bread machine in the order recommended by the manufacturer. Select White cycle; press start.
2. Remove loaf from the machine after the cycle is done and allow it to cool completely before slicing.

Nutritional Value (Amount per Serving):

Calories: 132; Fat: 2.09; Carb: 23.57; Protein: 4.2

Jo's Rosemary Bread

Prep Time: 10 mins

Cook Time: 40 mins

Additional time: 2 hrs 10 mins   Serves: 12

Ingredients:

- 1 cup water
- 3 tbsps olive oil
- 1 ½ tsps white sugar
- 1 ½ tsps salt
- ¼ tsp italian seasoning
- ¼ tsp ground black pepper
- 1 tbsp dried rosemary
- 2 ½ cups bread flour
- 1 ½ tsps active dry yeast

Directions:

1. Place ingredients in the pan of the bread machine in the order recommended by the manufacturer. Select White cycle; press start.
2. Remove loaf from the machine carefully after the cycle is done and allow it to completely cool.

Nutritional Value (Amount per Serving):

Calories: 129; Fat: 2.04; Carb: 23.36; Protein: 4.18

Dill Pickle Bread

Prep Time: 5 mins   Cook Time: 3 hrs   Serves: 12

Ingredients:

- 1 cup warm water (110 degrees f)
- 1 dill pickle, chopped
- 1 tbsp butter, softened
- 1 tbsp dried minced onion
- 1 tsp dried parsley
- ½ tsp dried dill weed
- ¼ tsp salt
- 3 ⅛ cups bread flour
- 2 tsps active dry yeast

Directions:

1. Place ingredients in the pan of the bread machine in the order suggested by the manufacturer.
2. Use the White, medium crust setting.
3. Cool the loaf when it's done before slicing.

Nutritional Value (Amount per Serving):

Calories: 147; Fat: 1.77; Carb: 27.27; Protein: 5.32

Bread Machine Cornbread – Sweet & Buttery

Prep Time: 5 mins   Cook Time: 1 hr 40 mins   Serves: 12

Ingredients:

- 1 1/4 cups milk (warm)

- 6 tbsps unsalted butter (sliced & softened)
- 2 eggs (lightly beaten)
- 1 1/2 cups all-purpose flour
- 1 cup yellow cornmeal – not self-rising cornmeal
- 1 cup white granulated sugar
- 1 tsp baking powder
- 1 tsp baking soda
- 1/2 tsp salt

Directions:

1. Soften the butter in a microwave.
2. Lightly beat the eggs.
3. Add milk, butter, eggs and then the rest of the ingredients into the bread pan.
4. Enter the bread machine settings (Cake, light crust, 2 lb) and press the start button. This setting should roughly last 1 hr 45 mins.
5. When the bread machine has finished baking the cornbread, remove the bread pan and place the bread pan on a wooden cutting board. Let the bread stay within the bread pan for 10 minutes before you remove it from the bread pan. Use oven mitts when removing the bread pan because it will be very hot!
6. After removing the cornbread from the bread pan, place the bread on a cooling rack. Use oven mitts when removing the bread. Let the cornbread cool down for 60+ minutes or it will be more likely to break/crumble when cut into slices.
7. Don't forget to remove the mixing paddle if it is stuck in the bread. Use oven mitts as the mixing paddle could be hot.

Nutritional Value (Amount per Serving):

Calories: 207; Fat: 9.91; Carb: 24.2; Protein: 5.59

Bread Machine Gingerbread

Prep Time: 10 mins   Cook Time: 1 hr 40 mins   Serves: 12

Ingredients:

- 1/2 cup vegetable oil (use a neutral flavored oil such as canola oil)
- 2 eggs (lightly beaten)
- 3/4 cup milk
- 1/4 cup molasses
- 1 cup light brown sugar (packed cup)
- 2 cups all purpose flour
- 1 1/2 tsps ground ginger

- 1 1/2 tsps ground cinnamon
- 1/2 tsp ground cloves (don't add too much as this can be a strong tasting spice)
- 1/2 tsp salt
- 1 tsp baking powder
- 1 tsp baking soda

Directions:

1. Lightly beat the eggs.
2. Pour the vegetable oil, milk & eggs into the bread pan and then add the remaining ingredients.
3. Enter the bread machine settings (Cake, light crust, 2 lb) and press the start button. The setting lasts roughly 1 hr 45 mins.
4. When the bread machine has finished baking the gingerbread, remove the bread pan and place it on a wooden cutting board (without removing the gingerbread from the bread pan). Use oven mitts when removing the bread pan because it will be very hot!
5. After removing the bread pan from the bread machine, you should let the gingerbread stay within the warm bread pan on the wooden cutting board for 10 minutes (as this finishes the baking process). Wear oven mitts.
6. After the 10 minute "Cooldown", you should remove the gingerbread from the bread pan and place the gingerbread on a wire cooling rack to finish cooling. Use oven mitts when removing the bread.
7. You should allow the gingerbread to completely cool before cutting. This can take up to 2 hours. Otherwise, the gingerbread will break (crumble) more easily when cut.

Nutritional Value (Amount per Serving):

Calories: 227; Fat: 11.97; Carb: 26.16; Protein: 4.7

Bread Machine Pumpkin Bread

Prep Time: 10 mins   Cook Time: 1 hr 40 mins   Serves: 12

Ingredients:

- 1 cup pumpkin puree – not canned pumpkin pie mix – 1 cup is approximately 8 oz.s of puree (not a full 15 oz. Pumpkin puree can)
- 2 eggs (large)
- 8 tbsps unsalted butter (sliced & softened) – or you can use 1/2 cup of a neutral-flavored vegetable oil (i.e. Canola oil or corn oil). See the tips section for more information.
- 2 cups all purpose flour
- 1/2 cup white granulated sugar

- 1/2 cup light brown sugar (packed)
- 1 tsp vanilla extract
- 1 tsp baking soda
- 1 tsp baking powder
- 1/2 tsp salt
- 1 tsp cinnamon – or you can add 2 tsps of your favorite pumpkin pie spice mix if you want more of a pumpkin pie flavor (versus mild cinnamon taste).

Directions:

1. Lightly beat the eggs.
2. Soften the butter in a microwave.
3. Add the pumpkin puree, eggs & butter (or oil) into the bread pan and then add the dry ingredients. Enter the bread machine settings (Cake, light crust) and press the start button.
4. When the bread machine has finished baking the bread, unplug the bread machine, remove the bread pan and place it on a wooden cutting board. Let the pumpkin bread stay within the bread pan (bread loaf container) for 10 minutes before you remove it from the bread pan. Use oven mitts when removing the bread pan because it will be very hot!
5. Optional – use a long wooden skewer to test if the pumpkin bread is completely cooked. Wear oven mitts as the bread pan will be hot. See the tips section for more details.
6. After the 10 minute "Cooldown", you should remove the pumpkin bread from the bread pan and place the pumpkin bread on a wire cooling rack to finish cooling. Use oven mitts when removing the bread.
7. Don't forget to remove the mixing paddle if it is stuck in the bread. Use oven mitts as the mixing paddle could be hot.
8. You should allow the pumpkin bread to completely cool before cutting. This can take up to 2 hours. Otherwise, the pumpkin bread will break (crumble) more easily when cut.

Nutritional Value (Amount per Serving):

Calories: 197; Fat: 12.33; Carb: 18.55; Protein: 3.04

Garden Vegetable Bread

Prep Time: 10 mins   Cook Time: 3 hrs   Serves: 16

Ingredients:

- 1/2 cup warm buttermilk (70 to 80 degrees f)
- 3 tbsps water (70 to 80 degrees f)
- 1 tbsp canola oil
- 2/3 cup shredded zucchini

- 1/4 cup chopped red sweet pepper
- 2 tbsps chopped green onions
- 2 tbsps grated romano or parmesan cheese
- 2 tbsps sugar
- 1 tsp salt
- 1/2 tsp lemon-pepper seasoning
- 1/2 cup old-fashioned oats
- 2-1/2 cups bread flour
- 1-1/2 tsps active dry yeast

Directions:

1. In bread machine pan, place all ingredients in order suggested by manufacturer.
2. Select White setting. Choose desired crust color and loaf size.
3. Bake according to bread machine directions (check dough after 5 minutes of mixing; add 1 to 2 tbsps of water or flour if needed).
4. Cool the loaf completely before slicing.

Nutritional Value (Amount per Serving):

Calories: 88; Fat: 1.61; Carb: 16.19; Protein: 3.62

Dark Kidney Bean Recipe

Prep Time: 5 mins   Cook Time: 3 hrs   Serves: 12

Ingredients:

- 1 cup milk
- 1 tbsp olive oil
- 1/4 cup onion, minced
- 1 1/2 tsp salt
- 2 1/2 cups bread flour
- 1 - 15 oz can dark red kidney beans, drained
- 2 packets or 4-5 tsp active dry yeast

Directions:

1. In a bread machine pan, place all ingredients in order suggested by manufacturer.
2. Select the White setting. Choose desired loaf size.
3. Bake according to bread machine directions (check dough after 5 minutes of mixing; add 1 to 2 tbsps water or flour if needed).
4. Cool the loaf completely before slicing.

Nutritional Value (Amount per Serving):

Calories: 144; Fat: 2.38; Carb: 24.98; Protein: 5.34

Bread Machine Spinach and Feta Bread

Prep Time: 15 mins   Cook Time: 3 hrs   Serves: 12

Ingredients:

- 1 cup water
- 2 tsps butter
- 3 cups flour
- 1 tsp sugar
- 2 tsps instant minced onion
- 1 tsp salt
- 1 ¼ tsps instant yeast
- 1 cup crumbled feta
- 1 cup chopped fresh spinach leaves

Directions:

1. Place all ingredients into the bread machine bowl except the yeast, cheese and spinach.
2. Place yeast in yeast hopper. Select the White setting.
3. With 10 minutes left in the last kneading cycle add spinach and cheese.
4. Cool the loaf completely and enjoy!

Nutritional Value (Amount per Serving):

Calories: 189; Fat: 5.02; Carb: 29.58; Protein: 6.29

Carrot Bread (Bread Machine)

Prep Time: 10 mins   Cook Time: 3 hrs   Serves: 12

Ingredients:

- 1 cup water
- 1 cup grated carrot
- 2 tbsps margarine
- 2 tbsps sugar
- ½ tbsp salt
- 4 cups bread flour
- 2 tsps active dry yeast

Directions:

1. Place water and carrot into blender and blend until you have a carrot juice.
2. Combine all ingredients (including the carrot juice) in the order given.
3. Select White and push start.
4. Important: Check the dough after about 5 minutes, if it's too wet then add a tbsp of flour at a time, if it's too dry then add a tbsp of water at a time, until dough forms a smooth round ball.

Nutritional Value (Amount per Serving):

Calories: 202; Fat: 2.86; Carb: 37.35; Protein: 6.52

Bread Machine Carrot Poppyseed Bread

Prep Time: 10 mins   Cook Time: 3 hrs   Serves: 12

Ingredients:

- 1/2 cup + 2 tbsps milk
- 2/3 cup finely shredded carrot
- 1 tbsp butter or margarine
- 2 tsps packed brown sugar
- 1 tsp poppy seeds
- 3/4 tsp salt
- 1-1/3 cups whole wheat flour
- 2/3 cup bread flour
- 1-1/2 tsps bread machine yeast

Directions:

1. Add ingredients to bread machine pan in the order suggested by manufacturer, adding carrot with milk. (carrots vary in moisture content. If dough is too dry or stiff or too soft or slack, adjust dough consistency-see adjusting dough consistency tip below.)
2. Recommended cycle: White cycle; medium color setting.
3. Adjusting dough consistency: After mixing for a few minutes, the ingredients should turn into a smooth ball around the kneading blade. If the dough appears too stiff or too soft, add more liquid or flour in 1 tsp increments, until the proper consistency is reached. Do not add more than 3 to 4 tsps liquid or flour.

Nutritional Value (Amount per Serving):

Calories: 79; Fat: 1.56; Carb: 14.12; Protein: 2.53

Bread Machine Whole Wheat Carrot Bread

Prep Time: 10 mins   Cook Time: 3 hrs   Serves: 12

Ingredients:

- 2 tbsps vegetable oil
- 4 tsps honey
- 2/3 cup cottage cheese
- 2 cups bread flour
- 2/3 cup whole wheat flour
- 1 cup grated carrots
- 1 tsp fine salt
- 2 tsps dill weed
- 3/4 tsp dry mustard
- 1 (0.25oz) package or 2 1/4 tsps active dry yeast

Directions:

1. Have liquid ingredients at 80 degrees f unless otherwise specified in your manual; all others at room temperature.
2. Add ingredients in order recommended by bread machine manufacturer. Select White and medium crust. Do not use the delay timer. Mixture is very dry as kneading begins. Check dough consistency after 10 minutes of

kneading. The dough should be in a soft, tacky ball. If it is dry and stiff, add water, 1/2 to 1 tbsp at a time. If it is too wet and sticky, add 1 tbsp of flour at a time.

3. When cycle is complete, carefully remove bread from pan; let cool on wire rack before slicing.

Nutritional Value (Amount per Serving):

Calories: 158; Fat: 3.52; Carb: 26.98; Protein: 5.36

Tomato Bread - Bread Machine

Prep Time: 15 mins   Cook Time: 3 hrs   Serves: 12

Ingredients:

- ¼ - ⅜ cup milk
- 6 tbsps tomato paste
- 1 egg
- 2 tsps olive oil
- ½ tsp salt
- 2 tsps sugar
- 2 cups bread flour
- ½ tsp italian seasoning
- 1 ½ tsps dried onion flakes
- ¼ tsp garlic powder
- ¼ tsp grated nutmeg
- 1 - 1 ½ tsp dry active yeast

Directions:

1. Place all ingredients in the order listed (unless your specific machine calls for it to be put in the opposite way).
2. Set the machine for: White setting, 1 lb, light crust.
3. When bread is done, remove from the pan and let cool for 1 hour before slicing.

Nutritional Value (Amount per Serving):

Calories: 152; Fat: 3.19; Carb: 25.78; Protein: 5.59

Bread Machine Easy Tomato Basil Bread

Prep Time: 10 mins   Cook Time: 3 hrs   Serves: 12

Ingredients:

- 2 cups tomato-basil flavored spaghetti sauce
- 2 tbsps grated parmesan cheese
- 3 to 4 cups bread flour
- 1 (0.25oz) package or 2 1/4 tsps active dry yeast

Directions:

1. Place spaghetti sauce, parmesan cheese, 3 cups bread flour and yeast in bread pan. Select White cycle and start machine. Keeping the lid of the

machine open, gradually add enough of the additional bread flour (1 tbsp at a time) until mixture forms a smooth, soft ball.

2. Close lid. When baking is complete, remove bread from machine as soon as possible. Cool on rack.

Nutritional Value (Amount per Serving):

Calories: 118; Fat: 5.34; Carb: 8.32; Protein: 9.13

Cracked Black Pepper Bread (Bread Machine)

Prep Time: 10 mins   Cook Time: 3 hrs   Serves: 12

Ingredients:

- 1 1/2 cups water (70 to 80 degrees f)
- 3 tbsps olive oil
- 3 tbsps sugar
- 2 tsps salt
- 3 tbsps minced chives
- 2 minced garlic cloves
- 1 tsp garlic powder
- 1 tsp dried basil
- 1 tsp cracked black pepper
- 1/4 cup grated parmesan cheese
- 4 cups bread flour
- 2 1/2 tsps active dry yeast

Directions:

1. Place all ingredients in bread machine pan in order suggested by manufacturer.
2. Select White setting.
3. Do not use time delay feature of your bread machine for this recipe.
4. Cool the loaf completely before slicing.

Nutritional Value (Amount per Serving):

Calories: 239; Fat: 4.76; Carb: 39.72; Protein: 9.27

Chapter 7: Cheese Breads

Cottage Dill Bread

Prep Time: 10 mins
Additional time: 2 hrs

Cook Time: 55 mins
Serves: 12

Ingredients:

- ⅔ cup warm water (110 degrees f)
- ⅔ cup cottage cheese
- 2 tbsps margarine
- 3 cups bread flour
- 1 tbsp white sugar
- 1 tbsp dry milk powder
- 1 tbsp dried minced onion
- 1 tbsp dill seed
- 1 tsp salt
- 1 ½ tbsps active dry yeast

Directions:

1. Place water, cottage cheese, margarine, flour, sugar, dry milk powder, onion, dill, salt, and yeast into a bread machine in the order listed, or follow the order recommended by the manufacturer if different.
2. Run the White cycle.
3. Remove loaf from the machine after the cycle is done and allow it to cool completely before slicing.

Nutritional Value (Amount per Serving):

Calories: 164; Fat: 3.24; Carb: 27.35; Protein: 6.34

Jalapeño Bread

Prep Time: 5 mins
Additional time: 2 hrs

Cook Time: 55 mins
Serves: 12

Ingredients:

- 1 cup warm water (110 degrees f)
- ½ cup shredded monterey jack cheese
- 6 tbsps chopped fresh jalapeño peppers
- 1 tsp salt
- 3 cups bread flour
- 2 tbsps white sugar
- ½ tbsp active dry yeast

Directions:

1. Place water, monterey jack cheese, jalapeño peppers, salt, flour, sugar, and yeast into a bread machine in the order listed, or follow the order recommended by your manufacturer if different.
2. Select White cycle.
3. Remove loaf from the machine after the cycle is done.

Calories: 164; Fat: 2.32; Carb: 29.57; Protein: 6.1

Cottage Cheese Bread

Prep Time: 5 mins   Cook Time: 3 hrs   Serves: 12

Ingredients:

- ½ cup water
- 1 cup cottage cheese
- 2 tbsps margarine
- 1 egg
- 1 tbsp white sugar
- ¼ tsp baking soda
- 1 tsp salt
- 3 cups bread flour
- 2 ½ tsps active dry yeast

Directions:

1. Add ingredients to your bread machine in the order suggested by the manufacturer, and start with the White setting.
2. You can use up to 1/2 cup more bread flour if dough seems too sticky.
3. Remove loaf from the machine after the cycle is done and allow it to cool before slicing.

Nutritional Value (Amount per Serving):

Calories: 182; Fat: 4.38; Carb: 27.27; Protein: 8.48

Italian Cheese Bread

Prep Time: 10 mins   Cook Time: 3 hrs   Serves: 12

Ingredients:

- 1 ¼ cups warm water
- 3 cups bread flour
- ½ cup shredded Pepperjack cheese
- 2 tsps Italian seasoning
- 1 tsp ground black pepper
- 2 tbsps grated parmesan cheese
- 2 tbsps brown sugar
- 1 ½ tsps salt
- 2 tsps active dry yeast

Directions:

1. Place warm water, flour, pepper jack cheese, italian seasoning, black pepper, parmesan cheese, brown sugar, salt, and yeast in the pan of a bread machine in the order suggested by the manufacturer.
2. Select White cycle, then start.
3. Remove loaf from the machine after the cycle is done and allow it to cool before slicing.

Nutritional Value (Amount per Serving):

Calories: 174; Fat: 2.09; Carb: 31; Protein: 7.11

Tangy Buttermilk Cheese Bread

Prep Time: 15 mins   Cook Time: 3 hrs   Serves: 12

Ingredients:

- 1 ⅛ cups buttermilk
- 3 cups bread flour
- 1 ½ tsps salt
- 1 ½ tsps white sugar
- ¾ cup shredded sharp cheddar cheese
- 1 ½ tsps active dry yeast

Directions:

1. Place ingredients in bread machine pan in the order suggested by the manufacturer.
2. Select White setting. Start.
3. Remove loaf from the machine after the cycle is done and allow it to cool before slicing.

Nutritional Value (Amount per Serving):

Calories: 204; Fat: 5.7; Carb: 28.75; Protein: 9.02

Cream Cheese Bread

Prep Time: 10 mins   Cook Time: 3 hrs   Serves: 12

Ingredients:

- ⅓ cup milk
- 1 cup cream cheese, diced
- ¼ cup margarine
- 1 egg
- 3 tbsps white sugar
- 1 tsp salt
- 3 cups bread flour
- 2 ½ tsps active dry yeast

Directions:

1. Place ingredients into the pan of the bread machine in the order suggested by the manufacturer. Select the White and light crust settings.
2. Remove the loaf from the pan and let it cool completely before slicing.

Nutritional Value (Amount per Serving):

Calories: 255; Fat: 11.33; Carb: 30.73; Protein: 7.69

Delicious Bread Machine Cheese Bread

Prep Time: 5 mins   Cook Time: 3 hrs   Serves: 12

Ingredients:

- 7/8 cup milk (lukewarm) – 7/8 cups of milk is equivalent to 3/4 cup and 2 tbsps of milk (if your measuring cup lacks the 7/8 marker)
- 3 tbsps unsalted butter (softened)
- 2 1/2 cups bread flour (not all purpose flour)
- 3/4 cup shredded cheese – use a strong tasting cheese (i.e. Extra sharp cheddar) or the bread may taste bland
- 3/4 tbsp light brown sugar
- 1 tsp salt
- 1 tsp bread machine yeast – not active dry yeast

Directions:

1. Soften the butter in a microwave.
2. Pour the milk & butter into the bread pan and then add the other ingredients (including the cup of cheese). Place the bread machine yeast in last and the yeast should not touch the liquid (until the bread machine is turned on and the ingredients start to be mixed together).
3. Optional – for greater flavor, you can also add diced jalapenos, minced & fried garlic cloves, thinly sliced chives/scallions (green stalks only) or italian seasoning. For best results, just pick one additional "Flavor" Ingredient (i.e. Just jalapenos). Place optional ingredient on the side of the bread pan and not on top of the yeast.
4. Enter the correct settings (White, light crust & 1.5 lb) and press the "start" Button.
5. Optional – after the final kneading cycle and before the baking cycle commences, sprinkle a little extra shredded cheese on top of the dough. For safety reasons, do not place your hands inside the bread machine.
6. Remove the bread pan when the bake is finished. Wear oven mitts as the bread pan will be very hot.
7. Remove the bread from the bread pan and place it on a cooling rack. Use oven mitts when handling the bread pan and bread as they will be very hot.

Nutritional Value (Amount per Serving):

Calories: 168; Fat: 5.88; Carb: 21.97; Protein: 6.25

Bread Machine - Easy Jalapeno Cheese Bread

Prep Time: 5 mins   Cook Time: 3 hrs   Serves: 12

Ingredients:

- 1 1/8 cups milk (lukewarm) – 1 1/8 cups of milk is equivalent to 1 cup and 2 tbsps of milk
- 4 tbsps unsalted butter (softened)
- 3 cups bread flour
- 1 cup shredded cheese
- 1 jalapeno pepper (diced into small bits)
- 1 tbsp brown sugar
- 1 tsp italian herbs
- 1 1/2 tsps salt
- 1 1/2 tsps bread machine yeast

Directions:

1. Pour the milk into the bread pan and then add the other ingredients including the diced jalapeno. Place the bread machine yeast in last and the yeast should not touch the liquid (until the bread machine is turned on and the ingredients start to be mixed together).
2. Enter the correct settings (White, 2 lb and light crust) and press the start button.
3. When the bread machine has finished baking the bread, unplug the bread machine. Remove the bread and place it on a cooling rack. Use oven mitts when removing the bread machine container (bread loaf pan) as it will be very hot!
4. After removing the bread, don't forget to remove the mixing paddle if it is stuck in the bread. Use oven mitts as the mixing paddle will be very hot coming out of the bread machine. Or wait until the bread is completely cooled and then remove the mixing paddle.

Nutritional Value (Amount per Serving):

Calories: 209; Fat: 6.83; Carb: 28.03; Protein: 8.32

Bread Machine Jalapeno Cornbread (with Cheese)

Prep Time: 10 mins   Cook Time: 1 hr 40 mins   Serves: 12

Ingredients:

- 1 cup milk
- 8 tbsps unsalted butter (softened)
- 2 eggs (lightly beaten)
- 1 1/2 cups yellow cornmeal
- 1 cup all-purpose flour
- 2 tbsps white granulated sugar
- 3 tsps baking powder (aluminum free)

- 1 tsp salt
- 1/4 cup jalapenos (diced into small chunks)
- 1 1/2 cups shredded cheddar cheese

Directions:

1. Soften the butter in a microwave.
2. Lightly beat the eggs.
3. Add milk, butter, eggs and then the rest of the ingredients into the bread pan. Try to follow the order of the ingredients listed above so that liquid ingredients are placed in the bread pan first and the dry ingredients second. Fyi - consider premixing the ingredients before adding the batter to the bread pan if you want to prevent flour sticking to the sides of the bread pan and/or finding small flour "Clumps" In the finished gingerbread.
4. Enter the bread machine settings (Ultra-fast, light crust, 2 lb) and press the start button.
5. When the bread machine has finished baking the cornbread, unplug your bread machine. Remove the bread pan and place the bread pan on a wooden cutting board. Let the bread stay within the bread pan for 10 minutes before you remove it from the bread pan. Use oven mitts when removing the bread pan because it will be very hot!
6. After removing the cornbread from the bread pan, place the bread on a cooling rack. Use oven mitts when removing the bread. Let the cornbread cool down for 60+ minutes or it will be more likely to break/crumble when cut into slices.
7. Don't forget to remove the mixing paddle if it is stuck in the bread. Use oven mitts as the mixing paddle could be hot.

Nutritional Value (Amount per Serving):

Calories: 206; Fat: 8.09; Carb: 28.34; Protein: 5.17

Pepper Jack Cheese Bread

Prep Time: 10 mins   Cook Time: 3 hrs   Serves: 14

Ingredients:

- 1 cup milk
- 3 cups bread flour
- 1 1/4 tsp salt
- 1 tbsp sugar
- 1 cup pepper jack cheese firmly packed
- 1/4 cup parmesan cheese grated
- 1 1/2 tsps active dry yeast

Directions:

1. Note that this is for a two-pound loaf of bread. Use the White setting with medium crust.
2. Follow the instructions that came with your bread machine in terms of

which ingredients to put in the machine first.

3. Check the dough after five or ten minutes of kneading. (pop the top of the bread machine and see how the dough looks.) it should be a smooth, round ball. If it's too dry, add liquid a tsp at a time until it looks ok. If it looks too wet, add flour a tbsp at a time until it looks ok.

Nutritional Value (Amount per Serving):

Calories: 166; Fat: 4.53; Carb: 23.64; Protein: 7.5

Pepper Cheese Loaf Bread Maker Recipe

Prep Time: 20 mins   Cook Time: 3 hrs 30 mins   Serves: 12

Ingredients:

- 2 and 1/2 cups + 1 tbsp bread flour
- 1/4 cup granulated white sugar
- 1 large egg, room temperature
- 3/4 tsp table salt
- 1 tbsp instant dry yeast
- 1/4 cup unsalted butter, melted
- 1/2 cup milk
- 1 tbsp + 1 tsp water
- 3/4 cup shredded cheese
- 1 and 1/2 tsp grounded black pepper (to taste)

Directions:

1. Firstly, melt the butter and ensure everything is at room temperature before mixing.
2. Place the ingredients in the sequence as specified by your bread maker's instruction manual. As a reference, I added everything at the bottom with the wet ingredients first before adding flour and then yeast!
3. Next, bake as per the bread maker machine specify. For mine, I used the French setting, which took approximately 3 hours of Cook Time.
4. You can add more cheese an hour to 1.5 hours before it rises and start cooking to coat the exterior with cheese.
5. Finally, serve and enjoy once you are done!

Nutritional Value (Amount per Serving):

Calories: 162; Fat: 7.11; Carb: 18.54; Protein: 5.7

Chapter 8: Sweet Breads

Bread Machine Challah I

Prep Time: 5 mins   Cook Time: 3 hrs   Serves: 12

Ingredients:

- ¾ cup milk
- 2 eggs
- 3 tbsps margarine
- 3 cups bread flour
- ¼ cup white sugar
- 1 ½ tsps salt
- 1 ½ tsps active dry yeast

Directions:

1. Add ingredients to the pan of the bread machine in the order suggested by the manufacturer.
2. Select the White setting and light crust settings. Start.
3. Carefully remove loaf from the machine with oven mitts after the cycle is done. Allow the bread to cool before slicing.

Nutritional Value (Amount per Serving):

Calories: 195; Fat: 6.45; Carb: 27.02; Protein: 6.92

Caraway Rye Bread (for the Bread Machine)

Prep Time: 10 mins   Cook Time: 4 hrs   Serves: 12

Ingredients:

- 1 ¼ cups lukewarm water (100 degrees f)
- 2 tbsps dry milk powder
- 1 tsp salt
- 2 tbsps brown sugar
- 2 tbsps molasses
- 2 tbsps butter
- ¾ cup whole wheat flour
- 1 ¾ cups bread flour
- ¾ cup rye flour
- 1 ½ tbsps caraway seeds
- 1 ¾ tsps active dry yeast

Directions:

1. Put lukewarm water, milk powder, salt, brown sugar, molasses, butter, whole wheat flour, bread flour, rye flour, caraway seeds, and yeast into the pan of a bread machine in the order suggested by the manufacturer.
2. Select the Whole-wheat setting and 2-pound loaf size.
3. Remove the bread from the machine with oven mitts after the cycle is done, and allow it to cool before slicing.

Nutritional Value (Amount per Serving):

Calories: 175; Fat: 2.96; Carb: 32.66; Protein: 5.51

Honey Wheat Oat Flour Bread Machine Bread

Prep Time: 10 mins   Cook Time: 3 hrs 20 mins   Serves: 10

Ingredients:

- ¾ cup water (80 degrees f)
- ¾ cup milk (80 degrees f)
- 1 ½ tbsps vegetable oil
- 6 tbsps honey
- 1 ½ tsps salt
- ¾ cup oats
- 1 cup oat flour
- 1 ¼ cups wheat flour
- 1 ¼ cups bread flour
- 1 ½ tsps active dry yeast

Directions:

1. Place warm water, milk, oil, honey, salt, oats, oat flour, wheat flour, bread flour, and yeast in the pan of a bread machine in the order listed.
2. Set cycle for White and light crust.
3. Remove the bread from the machine with oven mitts after the cycle is done, and allow it to cool before slicing.

Nutritional Value (Amount per Serving):

Calories: 240; Fat: 4.77; Carb: 44.62; Protein: 7.87

Chocolate Cinnamon Roll Bread Machine Bread

Prep Time: 10 mins   Cook Time: 3 hrs 30 mins   Serves: 12

Ingredients:

- ¼ cup water
- 1 cup milk
- 1 egg
- 1 tbsp vanilla extract
- 3 ⅓ cups bread flour
- ¼ cup sucralose and brown sugar blend
- 1 tsp salt
- 1 tsp ground cinnamon
- 1 tsp cocoa powder
- 1 ½ tsps active dry yeast
- 2 tbsps margarine, softened
- ½ cup peanut butter chips
- ¼ cup semisweet chocolate chips

Directions:

1. Place water, milk, egg, vanilla extract, bread flour, sucralose and brown sugar blend, salt, cinnamon, cocoa powder, yeast, and margarine respectively in the pan of a bread machine.
2. Select the White cycle with a light crust and 1.5 lb, and press start.
3. Add peanut butter chips and semisweet chips when the final knead cycle begins.
4. Cool bread for 10 to 15 minutes before slicing.

Nutritional Value (Amount per Serving):

Calories: 262; Fat: 7.97; Carb: 39.91; Protein: 7.42

Bread Machine Honey-Whole Wheat Bread

Prep Time: 10 mins   Cook Time: 45 mins   Serves: 16

Ingredients:

- 1 ½ cups warm water
- 2 tbsps butter
- ¼ cup raw honey
- 3 ½ cups whole wheat flour
- ¼ cup flaxseed meal
- ¼ cup vital wheat gluten
- 1 ½ tsps salt
- 1 ½ tbsps dry milk powder
- 2 tsps active dry yeast

Directions:

1. Place warm water, butter, honey, whole wheat flour, flaxseed meal, vital wheat gluten, salt, dry milk, and yeast in a bread machine in the order listed.
2. Run the White cycle, but adjust the Cook Timer to cut baking time down by 25 to 30 minutes. I time the bread and take it out when i see that it is not yet brown. If you like a crusty bread you may let it cook the entire time.
3. Remove loaf from the machine after the cycle is done.

Nutritional Value (Amount per Serving):

Calories: 156; Fat: 3.63; Carb: 25.49; Protein: 7.97

Fool-Proof Honey Whole Wheat Bread

Prep Time: 5 mins   Cook Time: 3 hrs   Serves: 10

Ingredients:

- 1 1/8 cups warm water (110 degrees f)
- 3 tbsps honey
- 2 tbsps vegetable oil
- 1 1/2 cups whole wheat flour
- 1 1/2 cups bread flour
- 1/3 tsp salt
- 1 1/2 tsps active dry yeast

Directions:

1. Place water, honey, oil, whole wheat flour, bread flour, salt, then yeast into a bread machine in the order listed, or follow the order recommended by the manufacturer if different.
2. Run Whole-wheat cycle, light color setting.
3. Remove loaf from the machine after the cycle is done, about 3 hours.

Nutritional Value (Amount per Serving):

Calories: 180; Fat: 3.79; Carb: 32.24; Protein: 5.71

Portuguese Sweet Bread I

Prep Time: 5 mins   Cook Time: 3 hrs   Serves: 12

Ingredients:

- 1 cup milk
- 1 egg
- 2 tbsps margarine
- ⅓ cup white sugar
- ¾ tsp salt
- 3 cups bread flour
- 2 ½ tsps active dry yeast

Directions:

1. Add ingredients mentioned above in order suggested by your manufacturer.
2. Select "Sweet" Setting.
3. Remove loaf from the machine after the cycle is done, and allow it to cool completely.

Nutritional Value (Amount per Serving):

Calories: 1.89; Fat: 5.31; Carb: 28.31; Protein: 7.33

Russian Black Bread

Prep Time: 15 mins   Cook Time: 3 hrs   Serves: 12

Ingredients:

- 1 ½ cups water
- 2 tbsps cider vinegar
- 2 ½ cups bread flour
- 1 cup rye flour
- 1 tsp salt
- 2 tbsps margarine
- 2 tbsps dark corn syrup
- 1 tbsp brown sugar
- 3 tbsps unsweetened cocoa powder
- 1 tsp instant coffee granules
- 1 tbsp caraway seed
- ¼ tsp fennel seed (optional)
- 2 tsps active dry yeast

Directions:

1. Place ingredients into the bread machine in order suggested by the manufacturer.
2. Use the Whole-wheat, medium crust settings.
3. After the baking cycle ends, remove bread from pan, place on a cake rack, and allow to cool for 1 hour before slicing.

Nutritional Value (Amount per Serving):

Calories: 179; Fat: 3.23; Carb: 33.49; Protein: 6.07

Essene Bread for the Bread Machine

Prep Time: 1 hr 30 mins

Additional time: 3 days 6 hrs 50 mins

Cook Time: 3 hrs

Serves: 15

Ingredients:

- ½ cup sprouted wheat berries, ground
- ¾ cup buttermilk
- 1 egg
- 2 tbsps maple syrup
- ½ tsp salt
- ⅓ tsp baking soda
- 2 tbsps vital wheat gluten
- 2 ¼ cups whole wheat flour
- 1 ½ tsps active dry yeast

Directions:

1. Beginning several days before you hope to be eating this bread, rinse 1/2 cup raw wheat berries in cool water; drain. Soak the berries with cool water in a large bowl. Cover the bowl with a plate or cloth, and allow the berries to soak at normal room temperature overnight or for about 12 hours. The berries will soak up a considerable amount of water. Drain the berries in a colander, cover the colander with a plate to prevent the berries from drying out, and set it in a place away from light. Rinse the berries about 3 times a day, and they will soon begin to sprout. In a couple of days the sprouts will reach their optimum length of about l/4 inch. Drain the sprouts and grind them in a blender or food processor.
2. Place ingredients in the pan of the bread machine in the order recommended by the manufacturer. Select whole Wheat-cycle and medium crust setting; press start.
3. If your machine has a raisin cycle, you can put the sprouts in at the beep for more intact sprouts. If not, the bread may have a mushy consistency.

Nutritional Value (Amount per Serving):

Calories: 112; Fat: 1.44; Carb: 20.28; Protein: 6.19

Hearty Multigrain Bread

Prep Time: 5 mins

Additional Time 2 hrs

Cook Time: 55 mins

Serves: 12

Ingredients:

- ¾ cup water
- 1 tbsp butter, softened

- 1 tsp salt
- 2 tbsps sunflower seeds
- 1 tbsp sesame seeds
- 1 tbsp flax seeds
- 1 tbsp millet
- 1 tbsp quinoa
- 1 cup bread flour
- 1 cup whole wheat flour
- 1 tbsp dry milk powder
- ¼ cup packed brown sugar
- 1 ½ tbsps bread machine yeast

Directions:

1. Place water, butter, salt, sunflower seeds, sesame seeds, flax seeds, millet, quinoa, bread flour, wheat flour, milk powder, brown sugar, and yeast into a bread machine in the order listed, or follow the order recommended by the manufacturer if different.
2. Run White cycle.
3. Remove loaf from the machine after the cycle is done and allow it to cool completely before slicing.

Nutritional Value (Amount per Serving):

Calories: 138; Fat: 3.52; Carb: 23.31; Protein: 4.25

Honey of an Oatmeal Bread

Prep Time: 5 mins   Cook Time: 3 hrs   Serves: 10

Ingredients:

- 1 cup water
- 1 tbsp vegetable oil
- ¼ cup honey
- 1 tsp salt
- ½ cup rolled oats
- 2 ⅓ cups bread flour
- 1 tsp active dry yeast

Directions:

1. Place ingredients in bread machine pan in the order suggested by the manufacturer.
2. Select light crust and White setting, and press start.
3. Remove loaf from the machine after the cycle is done and allow it to cool completely before slicing.

Nutritional Value (Amount per Serving):

Calories: 166; Fat: 2.25; Carb: 33.42; Protein: 4.82

Sweet Honey French Bread

Prep Time: 5 mins   Cook Time: 3 hrs   Serves: 12

Ingredients:

- ¾ cup water
- 2 tsps honey (optional)
- 2 tsps olive oil
- ⅔ tsp salt
- ⅔ tsp white sugar
- 2 cups bread flour
- 1 ½ tsps active dry yeast
- 1 tbsp honey (optional)

Directions:

1. Place ingredients in the pan of the bread machine in the order recommended by the manufacturer. Select White or French cycle; press start.
2. While bread is baking, drizzle with honey if desired.
3. Remove loaf from the machine after the cycle is done and allow it to cool before slicing.

Nutritional Value (Amount per Serving):

Calories: 110; Fat: 1.49; Carb: 20.71; Protein: 3.48

Seven Grain Bread II

Prep Time: 10 mins
Additional Time 1 hr 20 mins

Cook Time: 1 hr 30 mins
Serves: 8

Ingredients:

- 1 ⅓ cups warm water (110 degrees f)
- 1 tbsp active dry yeast
- 3 tbsps dry milk powder
- 2 tbsps vegetable oil
- 2 tbsps honey
- 2 tsps salt
- 1 egg
- 1 cup whole wheat flour
- 2 ½ cups bread flour
- ¾ cup 7-grain cereal

Directions:

1. Place ingredients in the bread machine pan in the order suggested by the manufacturer.
2. Select Whole-wheat cycle, and start.
3. Remove loaf from the machine after the cycle is done and allow it to cool before slicing.

Nutritional Value (Amount per Serving):

Calories: 308; Fat: 6.11; Carb: 54.56; Protein: 9.96

Oat-n-Honey Bread

Prep Time: 5 mins   Cook Time: 3 hrs   Serves: 10

Ingredients:

- 1 cup buttermilk
- 1 egg
- ¼ cup warm water (110 degrees f)
- 2 tbsps honey
- 1 ½ cups whole wheat flour
- 1 ½ cups all-purpose flour
- ½ cup quick cooking oats
- 2 tbsps vegetable oil
- 1 ½ tsps salt
- 1 ½ tsps active dry yeast

Directions:

1. Place ingredients into the bread machine in order suggested by the manufacturer.
2. Use the Whole-wheat settings. Start the machine.
3. Remove loaf from the machine after the cycle is done and allow it to cool before slicing.

Nutritional Value (Amount per Serving):

Calories: 201; Fat: 4.99; Carb: 33.16; Protein: 7.19

Oatmeal Applesauce Bread

Prep Time: 5 mins   Cook Time: 3 hrs   Serves: 12

Ingredients:

- ⅔ cup warm water
- 2 ¼ cups bread flour
- 1 tbsp white sugar
- 1 tbsp dry milk powder
- 1 tsp salt
- 1 tbsp butter
- ¼ cup rolled oats
- ¼ cup applesauce
- ½ tsp ground cinnamon
- 1 (0.25 oz.) package active dry yeast

Directions:

1. Place ingredients in the pan of the bread machine in the order recommended by the manufacturer. Select Whole-wheat cycle; press start.
2. Remove the loaf from the pan and cool it completely before slicing.

Nutritional Value (Amount per Serving):

Calories: 115; Fat: 1.63; Carb: 21.82; Protein: 3.79

Bread Machine – Butter Bread Recipe

Prep Time: 5 mins   Cook Time: 3 hrs   Serves: 12

Ingredients:

- 1 1/3 cups milk (lukewarm)

- 8 tbsps unsalted butter (sliced & softened)
- 3 cups bread flour
- 1 cup oatmeal (one minute oatmeal) – use dry oat flakes. Do not premoisten the oat flakes.
- 2 tbsps white granulated sugar
- 1 1/2 tsps salt
- 1 1/2 tsps bread machine yeast – not active dry yeast

Directions:

1. Add all ingredients starting with the milk into the bread machine "bucket" (bread pan).
2. Plug in bread machine. Enter the correct settings (2 lb, light crust & White) and press the "start" Button.
3. When the bread machine has finished baking the bread, unplug the bread machine. Remove the bread pan from the bread machine. Then remove the bread from the bread pan and place it on a cooling rack. Use oven mitts when removing the bread machine container (bread loaf pan) as it will be very hot!
4. After removing the bread, don't forget to remove the mixing paddle if it is stuck in the bread. Use oven mitts as the mixing paddle will be very hot coming out of the bread machine. Or wait until the bread is completely cooled and then remove the mixing paddle.

Nutritional Value (Amount per Serving):

Calories: 222; Fat: 7.35; Carb: 34.41; Protein: 7.34

Bread Machine Calzone Dough

Prep Time: 10 mins   Cook Time: 1 hr 40 mins   Serves: 16

Ingredients:

- 1 1/4 cups water (lukewarm)
- 3 tbsps olive oil
- 3 1/2 cups flour (all-purpose flour)
- 1 tbsp white granulated sugar
- 1 tsp salt
- 2 tsps bread machine yeast

Directions:

1. Add the water, olive oil and then the rest of the ingredients into the bread pan. You can make a little indent on top of the flour in order to avoid the yeast falling into the water (until the machine starts). Do not combine the salt with the yeast (as the salt can kill the yeast). Place the yeast & salt in separate parts of the bread pan.
2. Put your machine on the Dough setting and press the start button.
3. When your bread machine has finished, unplug the machine & pour the dough onto a cutting board. Wear oven mitts (as the bread pan/bread

machine may be hot). Sprinkle some flour on the cutting board (before you pour the dough) in order to avoid the dough sticking to the cutting board.

4. Divide the dough into two equal-sized balls (if you want to create two larger calzones) or four equal-sized balls (if want to create four smaller calzones).

5. With a rolling pin, roll out each ball of calzone dough into a round or oval shape. The depth of the rolled out dough should be roughly 1/4 inch thick.

Nutritional Value (Amount per Serving):

Calories: 113; Fat: 1.38; Carb: 21.25; Protein: 3.26

Bread Machine Chocolate Cake

Prep Time: 10 mins   Cook Time: 1 hr 40 mins   Serves: 12

Ingredients:

- 1 cup milk
- 12 tbsps unsalted butter – soften the butter into a liquid (i.e. Melt the butter in your microwave).
- 2 tsps vanilla extract
- 2 eggs
- 2 cups all-purpose flour
- 1 1/2 cups light brown sugar (packed cups)
- 1/2 cup cocoa powder natural unsweetened (not hot chocolate powder)
- 1 tsp baking powder
- 1 tsp baking soda
- 1 tsp salt
- 3/4 cup mini semi-sweet chocolate chips – regular sized chocolate chips are too heavy and sink in the batter

Directions:

1. Soften the butter in the microwave.
2. Add milk, butter, vanilla extract & eggs into a large mixing bowl. Mix together and then add dry ingredients. Stir ingredients until fully mixed. For best results, use a whisk or electric hand mixer (but for only a couple of minutes). Then mix in the chocolate chips with a large spoon. Fyi – premixing the ingredients before adding batter to the bread pan helps to prevent small flour "Clumps" In the finished cake. See tips below.
3. Pour the premixed batter into the bread pan.
4. Enter the correct bread machine settings (Cake, light crust, 2 lb.) and press the start button. This setting should last for roughly 1:40-1:55 hours.
5. When the bread machine has finished baking the cake, remove the bread pan and place it on a wooden cutting board. Use oven mitts when removing

the bread pan because it will be very hot!

6. Let the cake stay within the warm bread pan on a wooden cutting board for 10 minutes before you remove the cake from the bread pan. Wear oven mitts.

7. After the 10 minute "Cooldown", you should remove the cake from the bread pan and place the cake on a wire cooling rack to cool it completely. Use oven mitts when removing the bread.

Nutritional Value (Amount per Serving):

Calories: 317; Fat: 20.16; Carb: 28.98; Protein: 5.71

Bread Machine Cinnamon Bread (Chocolate Chip)

Prep Time: 10 mins   Cook Time: 1 hr 40 mins   Serves: 12

Ingredients:

- 3/4 cup milk
- 2 eggs (lightly beaten)
- 1/2 cup vegetable oil (use a neutral flavored oil such as canola oil)
- 1 tsp vanilla extract
- 2 cups all purpose flour
- 3/4 cup white granulated sugar
- 1/2 cup light brown sugar (packed cup)
- 1/2 tsp salt
- 1 tsp baking powder
- 1 tsp baking soda
- 1 tbsp ground cinnamon
- 1/2 cup mini chocolate chips

Directions:

1. Lightly beat the eggs.

2. Pour the milk, vegetable oil & eggs into the bread pan and then add the remaining ingredients.

3. Enter the bread machine settings (Cake, light crust, 2 lb) and press the start button. This setting lasts for roughly 1:40-1:55 hours.

4. When the bread machine has finished baking the cinnamon bread, remove the bread pan and place it on a wooden cutting board (without removing the cinnamon bread from the bread pan). Use oven mitts when removing the bread pan because it will be very hot!

5. After removing the bread pan from the bread machine, you should let the cinnamon bread stay within the warm bread pan on the wooden cutting board for 10 minutes (as this finishes the baking process). Wear oven mitts.

6. After the 10 minute "Cooldown", you should remove the cinnamon bread

from the bread pan and place the cinnamon bread on a wire cooling rack to finish cooling. Use oven mitts when removing the bread.

7. You should allow the cinnamon bread to completely cool before cutting. This can take up to 2 hours.

Nutritional Value (Amount per Serving):

Calories: 268; Fat: 16.21; Carb: 26.17; Protein: 5.12

Bread Machine Pound Cake

Prep Time: 10 mins   Cook Time: 1 hr 40 mins   Serves: 12

Ingredients:

- 3/4 cup unsalted butter – soften the butter into a liquid (i.e. Melt the butter in your microwave).
- 3 eggs (lightly beaten) – only large eggs. Not extra large or jumbo eggs.
- 2 cups all purpose flour
- 1 1/2 cups white granulated sugar
- 3 tsps baking powder – do not use baking soda! Baking soda is not the same as baking powder.
- 1/2 tsp salt
- 2 tsps vanilla extract

Directions:

1. Soften the butter in the microwave.
2. Lightly beat the eggs.
3. Add the butter & eggs into a large mixing bowl (not the bread pan). Mix together and then add the rest of the ingredients (except the confectioners sugar). Stir ingredients until fully mixed. For best results, use a whisk or electric hand mixer (but for only a couple of minutes). Fyi – you should premix the ingredients before adding the batter to the bread pan. This helps to prevent flour from sticking to the sides of the bread pan and/or finding small flour "Clumps" in the finished cake. See tips below.
4. Pour the premixed batter into the bread pan.
5. Enter the correct bread machine settings (Cake, light crust, 2 lb.) and press the start button. This setting lasts for roughly 1:40-1:50 hours
6. When the bread machine has finished baking the cake, unplug the bread machine, remove the bread pan and place it on a wooden cutting board. Use oven mitts when removing the bread pan because it will be very hot!
7. After removing the bread pan from the bread machine, you should let the cake stay within the warm bread pan on a wooden cutting board for 10 minutes (as this finishes the baking process) before you remove the cake from the bread pan. Wear oven mitts.

8. After the 10 minute "Cooldown", you should remove the cake from the bread pan and place the cake on a wire cooling rack to finish cooling. Use oven mitts when removing the bread.

9. You should allow the cake to completely cool before cutting. This can take up to 1-2 hours. Otherwise, the cake will break (crumble) more easily when cut.

10. Optional – after the cake has cooled, sprinkle some powdered confectioners sugar on the top of the cake.

Nutritional Value (Amount per Serving):

Calories: 278; Fat: 19.66; Carb: 20.53; Protein: 4.26

Bread Machine - Salt Crusted Bread

Prep Time: 5 mins   Cook Time: 3 hrs   Serves: 12

Ingredients:

- 1 1/3 cups water (warm)
- 4 tbsps butter (sliced)
- 3 cups flour
- 1 cup old fashioned oatmeal
- 1 tsp salt
- 1/3 cup brown sugar
- 1 1/2 tsps bread machine yeast
- 1/4 tsp - coarse food-grade salt (used to sprinkle on dough exterior)

Directions:

1. Add all ingredients starting with the water into the bread machine "bucket" (loaf pan).

2. Press the "Start" Button after entering the correct settings (2 lb, light crust & White).

3. After the bread machine has finished its final kneading cycle and before the baking cycle starts, gently sprinkle on some coarse salt on top of the dough. Don't go too crazy with the coarse salt or it will inhibit the yeast from rising.

4. After the bread machine has finished baking the bread, remove the bread and place it on a cooling rack. Use oven mitts when removing the bread machine container as it will be very hot!

Nutritional Value (Amount per Serving):

Calories: 261; Fat: 7.46; Carb: 43.57; Protein: 4.64

Seed Bread Recipe – Sunflower, Chia & Flax Seeds

Prep Time: 2 hrs 45 mins   Cook Time: 40 mins   Serves: 18

Ingredients:

- 1 1/8 cups milk (warm)
- 4 tbsps unsalted butter (sliced & softened)
- 3 cups bread flour
- 2 tbsps light brown sugar
- 1/4 cup sunflower seeds (unsalted & hulled) – feel free to adjust the sunflower, flax and chia seed amounts (as long as they equal 3/4 of a cup in total). See the tips section below.
- 1/4 cup flax seeds – not ground flax seeds (flax seed meal)
- 1/4 cup chia seeds
- 1 tsp salt
- 1 tsp instant yeast (bread machine yeast) – not active dry yeast

Directions:

1. Soften the butter.
2. Pour the milk & softened butter into the bread pan and then add the other ingredients. Place the instant yeast/bread machine yeast in last and the yeast should not touch the liquid (until the bread machine is turned on and the ingredients start to be mixed together by the bread machine). Fyi – many bakers like to make a crater/pocket in the top of the flour to hold the yeast so the yeast does not contact the liquid or salt in the bread pan.
3. Enter the correct settings (2 lb, light crust, White) and press the "Start" Button.
4. When the bread machine has finished baking the bread, unplug the bread machine and remove the bread pan from the bread machine. Wear oven mitts as the bread pan & bread machine will be hot.
5. Remove the bread from the bread pan and place the bread on a wire cooling rack. Use oven mitts when removing the bread as the bread & bread pan will be hot.
6. Optional – right after removing the bread from the bread pan (while the bread is still very hot), brush on 1 tbsp of melted butter on the top crust of the bread. This creates a more buttery top to the bread. Use a pastry brush to brush on the butter.
7. Let the bread cool on the wire cooling rack for 1-2 hours before cutting.

Nutritional Value (Amount per Serving):

Calories: 140; Fat: 3.86; Carb: 20.99; Protein: 5.22

Extra Soft Bread Machine Bread

Prep Time: 10 mins   Cook Time: 3 hrs   Serves: 12

Ingredients:

- 3/4 cup greek yogurt – you can also use sour cream
- 3/4 cup milk (warm)
- 4 tbsps unsalted butter (sliced & softened)
- 3 1/2 cups bread flour
- 3 tbsps white granulated sugar
- 1 1/4 tsps salt
- 1 1/4 tsps bread machine yeast (instant yeast) – not active dry yeast

Directions:

1. Soften the butter in your microwave.
2. Premix the greek yogurt (or sour cream). Fyi – this helps you to better measure the greek yogurt (or sour cream) in a measuring cup and helps evenly distribute any fruit if you use a fruit-flavored greek yogurt.
3. Add the greek yogurt (or sour cream), milk and butter into the bread pan and then add the remaining ingredients. Place the bread machine yeast in last and the yeast should not touch the liquid (until the bread machine is turned on and the ingredients start to be mixed together by the bread machine).
4. Enter the correct settings (light crust, 2 lb and White setting) and press the "Start" Button.
5. When the bread machine has finished baking the bread, unplug the bread machine and remove the bread pan from the bread machine. Wear oven mitts as the bread pan & bread machine will be hot.
6. Remove the bread from the bread pan and place the bread on a cooling rack. Use oven mitts when removing the bread as the bread & bread pan will be hot.
7. Optional – right after you remove the hot bread from the bread pan and place it on the cooling rack, you can use a pastry brush to brush a very light coat of melted butter on the top of the bread. This creates a more golden crust and adds even more buttery flavor. This works best when the bread is still hot. Fyi – do not use too much melted butter or it will run all over the sides of the bread. Also do not brush on after the bread has cooled down.
8. Let the bread cool on the cooling rack for 1-2 hours before cutting.

Nutritional Value (Amount per Serving):

Calories: 222; Fat: 5.91; Carb: 34.87; Protein: 7.03

APPENDIX RECIPE INDEX

Made in the USA
Columbia, SC
16 December 2024

49554144R00063